BIG BOSSMAN

Peter Ullian

BROADWAY PLAY PUBLISHING INC
224 E 62nd St, NY NY 10065-8201
212 772-8334 fax: 212 772-8358
BroadwayPlayPubl.com

First printing: June 2014
I S B N: 978-0-88145-597-7

Book design: Marie Donovan
Page make-up: Adobe Indesign
Typeface: Palatino
Printed and bound in the U S A

ABOUT THE AUTHOR

Peter Ullian's work for the stage has been produced off-Broadway, regionally, and internationally, and includes: HESTER STREET HIDEAWAY: A LOWER EAST SIDE LOVE STORY, produced off-Broadway by En Garde Arts; SIGNS OF LIFE (with lyrics by Len Schiff and music by Joel Derfner), produced off-Broadway by AMAS Musical Theatre, regionally at the Village Theatre and Victory Gardens Theater, and internationally at Divadlo DISK in the Czech Republic; FLIGHT OF THE LAWNCHAIR MAN (with music and lyrics by Robert Lindsey Nassif) directed by Harold Prince at the Prince Music Theater and the Ahmanson Theatre, and subsequently produced at Goodspeed Musicals and 37 Arts, as well as throughout the United States and in Liverpool and Edinburgh; ELIOT NESS IN CLEVELAND (with music and lyrics by Robert Lindsey Nassif), produced at the Directors Company, the Denver Center Theatre Company, and the Cleveland Playhouse; THE TRIUMPHANT RETURN OF BLACKBIRD FLYNT, produced at the Cleveland Public Theatre and Vertigo Theatre Factory; BIG CONSPIRACY, produced at HOME for Contemporary Theatre and Art and the Café Voltaire; STUCK IN LUXEMBOURG, produced at Theatre Winter Haven; and BIG BOSSMAN, produced at the Cleveland Public Theatre. FLIGHT OF THE LAWNCHAIR MAN is published and licensed by

Theatrical Rights Worldwide, and continues to be produced throughout the United States. The original cast recording of LAWNCHAIR MAN is available on the album *3hree* from DRG Records. Ullian's play NEW AMERICAN CENTURY was developed at the Lark Play Development Center and at 4th Wall at the Beacon. His play BLACK FIRE WHITE FIRE was presented at Jewish Plays Project's OPEN: The Festival of New Jewish Theater at the 14th Street Y, and his follow-up play, SPIRIT IN THE SKY, was developed at the Hollins Playwright's Lab and at Jewish Plays Project. His play DANCING NAKED IN THE LINE OF DUTY was developed at the American Theater Company. He wrote book and lyrics for the ten-minute musical THE DREAMS YOU CHOOSE (music by Scott Ramsburg), which premiered as part of the Mill Mountain Theatre's Overnight Sensations. His awards for dramatic writing include the Roger L. Stevens Award from the Kennedy Center/A T & T Fund for New American Plays for IN THE SHADOW OF THE TERMINAL TOWER; two Gilman & Gonzalez-Falla Musical Theatre Foundation Commendation Awards; and two N E A production grants (for FLIGHT OF THE LAWNCHAIR MAN and SIGNS OF LIFE.) He also received a Barrymore Award nomination for Outstanding New Play for FLIGHT OF THE LAWNCHAIR MAN. His screenplays include *Justice* (Paramount); *Denial* (Zeal Pictures); and *A Beginner's Guide to Armed Robbery* (Hollywood Pictures/ Windancer Films). His original screenplay *Survivors* was optioned by Oscar-winning producer Mark Johnson, and subsequently optioned by actor Alfred Molina and director Mark Rydell. His fiction includes *Owen's Blood* (Cemetery Dance and Hardboiled), *The Vietnamization of Centauri V* (DAW Books anthology Star Colonies), and *Ribbons and Tin*, (Cemetery Dance, paper and ebook.). He is a contributor to *The Field*

Guide to Poetic Playwriting, published by Rose Metal Press. He has taught creative writing at SUNY Old Westbury and playwriting at the M F A Hollins Playwrights Lab. He has been profiled in *The Jewish Week, The Cedar Rapids Gazette,* the *Cleveland Plain Dealer,* and *The Los Angeles Times.* A member of the Dramatists Guild, he is a graduate of Oberlin College and the University of Iowa's Playwrights Workshop. He lives in the Hudson Valley with his wife and two children.

BIG BOSSMAN was first performed at the Cleveland Public Theatre (James Levin, Artistic Director). It opened on 17 November 1989. The cast and creative contributors were:

RIFF .... Bruce Dunn
BIFF ....Dan Sobel
ROSE...Cynthia Wasseen
VIOLET .... Lisa Paciorek
BIG BOSSMAN .... Barry Saxon
FRANCIS... William True
CURTIS ....Rohn Thomas

Director..Rohn Thomas
Set design ....R C Naso
Costume design.. Terry Gelzer
Lighting design .... Dennis Dugan

The characters RIFF *and* BIFF *were subsequently renamed* RAY *and* BILLY.

Additionally, Lisa Portes directed an earlier developmental workshop of BIG BOSSMAN as part of Cleveland Public Theatre's the Sixth Festival of New Plays. This edition incorporates much of the excellent dramaturgical advice she provided then and subsequently, and from which the play has continued to benefit since its first incarnation.

CHARACTERS & SETTING

RAY, *a young man in his mid-twenties.*

BILLY, *his younger brother, early twenties. He is* not, *as his siblings suggest, developmentally disabled.*

ROSE, *their older sister. About two years older than* RAY.

CURTIS, *their father. A big, stinking drunk. Older than a man with children their ages is expected to be.*

VIOLET, *a prostitute. About* BILLY'S *age. Russian accent.*

BIG BOSSMAN, a *very slick gangster and* VIOLET'S *pimp. A big guy. Sort of a cross between a yuppie Sidney Greenstreet and Kevin Spacey. He is nattily dressed and carries a walking stick. He behaves like a hybrid of a contemporary man and a man from a different era. His manners are impeccable until they're not. Age is hard to determine.*

FRANCIS, *his bodyguard. Tall. Looks like Boris Karloff. Talks like Don King. Likewise, his age is hard to figure.*

Scene & Time: The kitchenette/living room area in a small apartment in the city. 2009, during the worst days of the Great Recession.

NOTE ON MUSIC:

It is suggested in the script that Jimmy Reed's or Elvis Presley's rendition of Big Bossman *be used at two points during the play. This suggestion does not imply rights to the use of the song or the recordings, which must be acquired by the producers, or substituted with another song. If rights are acquired, explore the possibility of using Jimmy Reed's version during the opening and Elvis Presley's at the end, or vice versa.*

NOTE ON CASTING:

Most of the characters can be played by actors of any ethnicty. BILLY, CURTIS, RAY, *and* ROSE *should be believably from the same family, although their mother, who is deceased and does not appear in the play, could have been from any ethnicity.* VIOLET, *however, should look like someone from Vladivostok.*

Scene One

(Home)

(In the darkness, beginning at an audible point and rising in volume, someone singing, preferably Luther Dixon's Big Bossman. *If possible, Elvis Presley's studio recording would be ideal, but not the live 1968* Singer T V Special *recording. Also, check out the Jimmy Reed version. About half-way through the song, when the volume is up to the midpoint, a match flickers on stage. The lights begin to come up slowly, following the rising volume of the music.* RAY *stands, nervous and jittery, but holding himself stiffly.)*

(The second the songs ends, BILLY *comes charging on-stage, holding his neck. There is blood running down his arm and face. His clothes are liberally splattered with it.)*

BILLY: Christ, Ray!

RAY: OmiGod—

BILLY: Christ, I'm bleedin'!

RAY: What happened?

BILLY: Jesus, Jesus, Jesus, look at all this blood!

RAY: Lemmie see—

BILLY: I'm finished—

RAY: Lemmie see, f'Christ—

BILLY: They must've unplugged a major artery, Ray.

RAY: Lemmie see, damnit!

BILLY: I think it's too late, Ray!

RAY: Shut up a sec. Lemmie see. Maybe it's not so bad.

BILLY: It's bad, Ray, it's bad!

RAY: Take your hand away—

BILLY: It's bad, Ray, it's real bad! I'm a goner. I know it! I'm blacking out, Ray! I'm blacking out!

RAY: Lemmie take a look—

BILLY: Have you ever seen so much blood?

RAY: Yes.

BILLY: When?

RAY: Well, *Saving Private Ryan*, for one.

BILLY: That was a whole fuckin' war, though, Ray! An entire fucking continental invasion! I'm just one guy here, Ray! One lousy guy!

RAY: Lemmie see your neck.

(BILLY lowers his head. RAY examines.)

RAY: You're not bleedin'—

BILLY: What'd'ya mean, I'm not bleedin'? What do you call all this blood? This is not ketchup, Ray! This is not red dye number four! This is blood! This is a whole lotta blood!

RAY: What I am saying is that you are not bleeding any more. The bleeding, which had been previously occurring, has now stopped.

(Beat)

BILLY: Christ, I sure was scared for a minute there, Ray.

RAY: Lemmie fix you up.

BILLY: I thought I was gonna die.

RAY: Lemmie fix you up. *(He takes a little first aid kit and attends to BILLY's wound.)* What the fuck happened here anyway, Billy?

BILLY: Nothin'.

RAY: Don't play with me right now, O K Billy? I mean, you come in here, making me think some wild dog or somethin' just tore your throat open, and then you play with me? Just tell me what happened.

BILLY: Bunch a fuckin' punks, Ray, tried to rip me off.

(Beat)

RAY: What'd you do to 'em, Billy?

BILLY: Do to 'em? I couldn't do nothin' to 'em. There was too many of 'em to do nothin'. I just tried to duck, and, like, protect my balls, Ray. Duck an' cover, that's all.

RAY: What'd you do to make 'em mad?

BILLY: I…what did I…you're askin' me what I…how can you even ask me that, Ray?

RAY: Don't play your fucking games with me, Billy. I'm sick of games, O K? Just tell me. What'd you do?

BILLY: Why is it—huh?—why is it that it's always gotta be me? Huh?

RAY: Because—

BILLY: Why is it that I always gotta have done something wrong?

RAY: Because you—

BILLY: Why is it that it's always gotta be my fault?

RAY: Because—

BILLY: I'm the one with the blood all over myself, y'know!

RAY: I—

BILLY: I'm the one who had his jugular sliced open, y'know!

RAY: You didn't—

BILLY: I'm the one who nearly died, y'know!

RAY: You didn't—

BILLY: I'm the victim here, y'know!

RAY: You—

BILLY: So, how come it's always gotta be me?

RAY: Because—

BILLY: How come it's always gotta be my fault?

RAY: Because you—

BILLY: How come it's never the other guy?

RAY: Because—

BILLY: How come I always gotta be the one to blame?

RAY: Because you're a total fuck up, Billy! You fuck things up right and left and all over the fuckin' place! You fuck things up everywhere you go! You're a fucking national disaster area, Billy! I'm gonna fucking call up fucking FEMA and see about getting myself some fucking money, you're such a fucking disaster. All you ever do is fuck things up!

(Beat)

BILLY: Not always.

RAY: Always!

BILLY: That's not fair!

RAY: Billy—that's like, way past fair. That's like, extremely generous.

BILLY: Fuck you.

RAY: Are you gonna tell me what happened?

BILLY: No.

RAY: One more chance here, Billy. One more chance, and then I fuckin' lose my temper.

BILLY: It was *The Good the Bad and the Ugly*, is the thing, Ray.

RAY: O K, is that, like, a reference to the Clint Eastwood, Sergio Leone movie, or a description of the kids who cut you?

BILLY: And Eli Wallach. And Lee Van Cleef, too. Don't forget him. He was in *The Man Who Shot Liberty Vallance*, too. One of Lee Marvin's henchmen.

RAY: So, we're talking about the movie.

BILLY: Yeah, the movie, not *Liberty Vallance, The Good, the Bad, and the Ugly,* which I bought from these guys on the corner just, like, yesterday.

RAY: Billy, how many times have I told you, don't play three card monte and don't buy movies on the street.

BILLY: But it was *The Good, the Bad, and the Ugly*, Ray. *(He sings the theme song)*
Doo-do-lo-de-loo…dum, dum, dum.
Doo-do-lo-de-loo…dum, dum, dum!

RAY: Do want to know how much patience I've got left with you right now, Billy? Do want me to, like, quantify it for you somehow? Like, can you see the space between my fingers, here, 'cause that's about all there is, O K? *(He holds his thumb and index finger up. There is no space between them.)*

(Beat)

BILLY: So, I bought the fuckin' movie, and it's on fucking video tape, which is cool, because it's cheaper than D V D and we don't have a fucking Blu-ray machine, so I went to the library to watch it, 'cause, you know, they give you headphones and, like, a booth, and you can watch a movie on videotape there for like, free, 'cept, like, they don't like it if they see you in there watchin' porn, but that wasn't the case here, this was a classic Western, Ray, a classic—

RAY: I know that, Billy, what—

BILLY: O K. So, like, I'm sitting there watching the movie and then, like, guess what happens right at the climax, when Lee Van Cleef, Clint Eastwood, and Eli Wallach are all squaring off against each other in the graveyard?

RAY: I don't have to guess. I know. Because I've seen the movie.

BILLY: WELL, NOW, THAT'S ONE YOU GOT OVER ME BECAUSE I DON'T FUCKIN' KNOW SHIT ABOUT HOW THE FUCKIN' MOVIE ENDS AND HOW THE FUCK WOULD I FUCKIN' KNOW THAT GIVEN THE FACT THAT THE FUCKIN' TAPE RAN OUT JUST AT THAT MOMENT WITH A BIG FUCKIN' CLICK, AND THEN JUST GOES REWINDING ITS FUCKIN' SELF?

RAY: Billy, we've seen the fuckin' movie before.

BILLY: Well, that's not exactly the fuckin' point, is it, Ray? The fuckin' point is that I wanted to watch the fuckin' movie NOW!

RAY: You don't buy movies on the street, Billy. That's a known fact. It's like chewing gum you find on the bottom of a park bench. It's a dumb thing to do. Normal human beings who live in a civilized society do not do that.

BILLY: But it was only two bucks!

RAY: You're such a fuckin' retard, Billy! What did you do? You went and asked for your money back, didn't you? You are such a fuckin' retard!

BILLY: Yeah, except it wasn't the same two guys.

RAY: Oh, Billy…don't tell me…

BILLY: Well, they all know each other, Ray! I mean, they all work for the same fuckin' criminal conspiracy!

RAY: Who says they all know each other, Billy? Where did you pick up that little nugget of information? I mean, Jesus, Billy, you redefine the word "asinine".

BILLY: I couldn't even define the word "asinine" the first time.

RAY: Just stop fucking around. Or we're both gonna be out of a job.

BILLY: Fuck the job.

RAY: *(Harshly)* Don't say that. I'm fuckin' serious. Don't you say that ever again. We need this job, Billy. We need it so bad it's givin' me an ulcer, O K? I gotta take Pepto-fuckin'-Bismol just to get out the door in the morning. I got some kinda fucking acid relfluxitation thing in my fuckin' throat, here, all the time. Have you seen what it's like out there? We were hurting even before those fuckers at Lehman Brothers screwed the pooch and the economy went to shit. Now, it's like fucking Armageddon out there, people are getting fired like fuck, and the ones with jobs are getting paid shit.

BILLY: This job sucks.

RAY: We need this job.

BILLY: Fuck this job.

(RAY suddenly cracks BILLY a good one across the mouth with the back of his hand.)

BILLY: Christ! Is that any way to treat a wounded man!?!?

RAY: What did I tell you, Billy?

BILLY: I'm gonna bleed again, y'know, thanks to you!

RAY: What did I tell you, Billy?

BILLY: *(Putting his hand to his bandage)* I think that I'm bleedin' again, Ray!

RAY: What did I tell you, Billy?

BILLY: Fuck you.

(RAY *slaps* BILLY *again.*)

RAY: One more time: What did I tell you, Billy?

(Beat)

BILLY: That we need the job.

RAY: What else?

BILLY: Not to knock the job.

RAY: What else?

(Beat)

BILLY: To stop fucking around.

RAY: Are you gonna do these things, Billy?

(Beat)

BILLY: Yes.

RAY: Good. Now get out of these bloody clothes before Rose sees you.

(RAY *moves away from* BILLY, *and gets a garbage bag.*)

(*As he speaks,* BILLY *strips naked.*)

BILLY: You didn't have to hit me, Ray. *(Beat)* You're always hittin' me. Like you got some kinda right. I'm not a kid, y'know, anymore. You can't beat me up like you could when we was kids, y'know. I don't have to take it no more. Not if I don't want to.

(Beat)

RAY: Put your clothes in the garbage bag.

BILLY: You're going to throw away my clothes?

RAY: You want Rose to see them and freak out?

(Beat. BILLY *puts the clothes in the garbage bag.)*

RAY: Now wet a washcloth and bring it to me.

(BILLY *goes to the bathroom. We hear water running and he comes out with a wet washcloth.*)

BILLY: Obama's president now. Maybe he can make things better.

(RAY *takes the washcloth, and wipes blood from* BILLY's *skin.*)

RAY: That fucker's not going to make anything better. Best we can hope for is that he's going to stop it from getting any worse. But we want things to be better, no one's gonna help us do that but us taking what's out there. We want things to be better, no one's gonna help us do that but us taking what's out there for our own.

BILLY: Maybe he will. Maybe he will finally make things better. *(Beat)* I saw Dad this mornin', ya' know. He was leavin' the bathroom.

(Beat)

RAY: What'd he say?

BILLY: He asked if I had a job yet.

RAY: What'd you say?

BILLY: I told him yeah.

(Beat)

(End of Scene)

Scene Two

(Home)

*(*ROSE *appears. She is naked except for rubber gloves, rubber rain boots, safety goggles, and a surgical mask. She carries a toilet plunger, a bucket, a wrench. She is flushed and sweaty. Her hair is a disaster. She stands by the fish tank, takes off her surgical mask, and talks to the fish.)*

ROSE: Fuck you. You fucking fish. You fucking fishy fuck. You fucking fish-fucking fishy fucker. *She notices a single shaft of sunlight coming in through the dirty, greasy window. She stares at it for a few moments. Then she throws the toilet plunger, wrench, safety goggles, and surgical mask in the bucket, and goes and stands in the ray of light. She closes her eyes for a moment, feeling the heat from the ray of sun. She occasionally changes her position in relation to the sunlight so that she can feel the light fall upon her face, her back, etcetera. As she is doing this, she opens her eyes and looks at the fish.)* I don't know why you hang out here, you fucking fishy fucker. If I were you, I'd get the hell outta this shithole. I'd play dead until they flushed me down the toilet, and then I'd slosh my way through the sewage until I came out into the harbor. Then I'd swim out past the tugboats and the barges and the ferries. I'd swim 'till I got to the beaches on the big island. I'd look at all them rich folk comin' outta their big, Frank Lloyd Wright/Philip Johnson houses, wearing their blue turtle-necks and white pants, smoking big pipes, puffing pricey puffs of puffy white smoke, and drinking gin and tonics. I'd watch them get in their big, thirty-foot sailboats and sail them around the bay. And then I'd move on. I'd move on until I felt the first warm currents from Mexico. And I'd follow them south. Down south to the Gulf of Mexico. I wouldn't stop until all around me was clear blue Caribbean water. Warm water. Water that feels like the sun on your

back. I'd watch the tropical fish swim around. I'd see
the pearl-divers diving for pearls. I'd watch ships and
planes disappear in the Bermuda Triangle. I'd swim
around the wreck of a 16th century Spanish Galleon,
gold coins spilling out of its guts. I'd swim through the
underwater ruins of ancient Aztec temples. I'd look
at the ghost of Ernest Hemmingway landing a striped
Marlin. I'd watch Panamanian drug-smugglers racing
by on speed boats. I'd swim through coral reefs. I'd
swim around Cuba. I'd never stop swimming. *(Beat)*
I certainly wouldn't fucking hang around here. You
fucking fishy fuck fish-fucking fishy fucker.

(Beat)

(CURTIS is heard calling from off-stage.)

CURTIS: Rose! You should go on this show!

(Beat)

ROSE: *(She closes her eyes and takes a big breath before
responding as nicely as she can:)* Which show is that,
Dad?

CURTIS: This one!

ROSE: Which one?

CURTIS: The millionaire one!

(Beat)

ROSE: *Who Wants to be a Millionaire*?

CURTIS: Not that one! That one was cancelled!

ROSE: Which one, then?

CURTIS: The other one!

ROSE: Which other one?

CURTIS: The other millionaire one!

ROSE: *Jeopardy*?

CURTIS: Certainly not!

ROSE: *Win Ben Stein's Money?*

CURTIS: That was cancelled, too! And you can't win more than five thousand dollars on that show! How does that qualify as a millionaire show? That is not even remotely within striking distance of a millionaire show!

ROSE: *Survivor?*

CURTIS: Don't be absurd!

ROSE: Which millionaire show, then?

CURTIS: The one with the Gulf-War Veteran and the Motivational Speaker!

(Long pause, as ROSE thinks, hard.)

ROSE: *Who Wants to Marry a Multi-Millionaire?*

CURTIS: That's the one! That's the one!

ROSE: Dad—

CURTIS: You should go on that show!

ROSE: Dad!

CURTIS: You're a smart, attractive girl! You talk good and, yes, while you are a mite awkward and gawky on your feet, there's no reason why you could not learn to walk with grace and poise in heels and a swimming suit! You could do very well on that show! There's no reason you can't marry a multi-millionaire! There are lots of multi-millionaires out there, with oil fields and shale fracking enterprizes and fat private military contracts, and they're all going on television shows in the hope of getting married to a nice girl like you! You could marry one, and then have a lot of money! And then we could move into a big house, with a swimming pool, and I could have my own wing, the East Wing, with Blu-ray and flat-screen high definition television and all the premium H D cable channels, instead of just basic!

ROSE: We don't even get basic anymore, Dad. The cable got cut off.

CURTIS: Well, then, someone forgot to mention that to my T V, because I still get C-Span and M T V! And the *Who Wants to Marry a Multi-Millionaire* channel!

ROSE: Are you sure that metal plate in your head isn't picking up satellite broadcasts?

CURTIS: Don't you make fun of my disability! I got this metal plate fighting for my country and ensuring your God-Given Constitutionally Protected right to sass your father like the ungrateful little bitch-child you are!

ROSE: You got it by falling off your bar stool and onto your head!

CURTIS: Go ahead! It's a free country! Sass me all you want! That's what I fought and suffered these disabling injuries for! I'll just turn up the volume and watch *Who Wants to Marry a Multi-Millionaire*!

ROSE: Dad, they only did that show once, like, over a decade ago! They aren't doing it any more!

(Beat)

CURTIS: That's not so. I see that show on all the time! Twice a day, at least. They're marrying all these young women off to multi-millionaires all the time. I'm telling you, you should get in on that action! I'm watching it right now with the sound turned off!

(Beat)

ROSE: I think you should change the channel. Switch to C-Span.

CURTIS: I don't watch C-Span, for Christsakes! I said I get C-Span, not that I watch C-Span! I'm not a college educated upwardly mobile individual like yourself.

ROSE: I'm not a college educated upwardly mobile individual like myself, either, in case you need to be reminded!

CURTIS: Don't get smart with me, young lady! It's not my fault I've been stricken with battle injuries and denied my government disability that I'm entitled to as a veteran of foreign wars in good standing! I worked hard all my life!

ROSE: Mom worked hard all her life! You sat on your ass all your life!

CURTIS: Don't you throw your mother in my face, young lady! No one could live up to your mother! *(Beat. Weepily:)* Your mother was a saint! *(Beat)* You should marry one of these intercommercewebinaires. Everyone thinks the economy went down the toilet because the prices of houses went down the toilet, but let me ask you this: Are people still sending e-mails? Are they still downloading music? Of course they are! You think that stuff is free? What did those guys who invented FaceSpace and MyTube walk away with? Kajillions! The technology revolution is still making millionaires! Marry one! Stop wasting my time! Get on with it! Send them a postcard and get on that show and marry a multi-millionaire and get me out of this shithole already! What are you waiting for?

ROSE: *(To herself:)* Fucking idiot. *(She stands for a moment longer, in silence. Then she goes to a kitchen cabinet, takes out a bottle of whiskey, takes it to the sink, and pours it all out. Then she goes to the fishtank and picks up the bucket. She pauses for a moment, thinks. Then she grabs a small net, and scoops out the fish. She goes off stage with the bucket, the net, and the fish.)*

(Enter BILLY *and* RAY.*)*

BILLY: We're home.

RAY: The working men are home.

(They look at the fish bowl. Beat)

BILLY: Where's Elvis?

(The sound of a toilet flushing is heard from off stage.)

(After a moment, ROSE enters, now fully dressed, her hair pulled back.)

BILLY: We're home!

ROSE: I see that.

RAY: The working men are home.

BILLY: Where's Elvis?

ROSE: Elvis has left the building. Did you work today?

BILLY: Did we work today?

RAY: We worked today.

BILLY: Did we ever work today!

ROSE: Did you get paid?

BILLY: Did we ever!

RAY: We got paid.

ROSE: How much?

RAY: Enough.

BILLY: A ton!

ROSE: How much?

BILLY: More than you can count!

ROSE: More than you can count, maybe. Hand it over.

(RAY hands ROSE some bills. She counts them.)

ROSE: Where's the rest of it?

RAY: We kept some.

ROSE: What for?

RAY: Cigarettes.

ROSE: You don't need that many cigarettes.

RAY: We might.

BILLY: You never know.

RAY: It's cheaper if you buy 'em by the carton.

ROSE: Give it here.

RAY: We need it. We got plans.

ROSE: Bullshit. You never had a plan in your life. Hand it over.

(Beat. RAY *hands over the rest of the money.)*

BILLY: I hate this job.

RAY: It's the easiest money you'll ever make.

BILLY: I don't like Francis.

ROSE: Who's Francis?

RAY: He's the Big Bossman's man. His right hand man. His aide de camp. His major domo.

ROSE: What's wrong with him?

RAY: Strange guy, is all.

BILLY: I don't like the Big Bossman.

RAY: He likes you.

BILLY: He does?

RAY: Yep.

ROSE: The boss likes Billy?

RAY: Not just any boss. The BIG Boss. The Big Bossman. The guy who runs everything this part a' town. A big important guy.

BILLY: He likes me?

RAY: Yep.

BILLY: No, he don't.

RAY: Yes, he does.

BILLY: Yeah?

RAY: He told me.

BILLY: Fuck off—

RAY: Swear to God.

BILLY: Honest?

RAY: Honest. He said to me, "Your brother Billy does the job and keeps his mouth shut."

(Beat)

BILLY: That doesn't exactly sound like a ringing endorsement, Ray.

RAY: Wait. He also said "He knows how to stay in his place. How to do as he's told. I like that in my employees."

BILLY: That still doesn't sound overly-enthusiastic.

RAY: And he said to me "I think your brother's got some brains. I like an employee with brains. He might have a future with us."

BILLY: Honest?

RAY: Honest.

BILLY: He thinks I got brains?

RAY: I don't know where he got the idea, but he's convinced of it.

BILLY: He thinks I'm intelligent?

RAY: I tried to set him straight, but he wouldn't listen to me.

BILLY: Weird…

RAY: That's how I feel.

ROSE: That's pretty good luck, Billy. You can go places with him.

BILLY: Yeah, whatever.

ROSE: You two do right by him, and he might help fix you up in a business.

BILLY: Yeah. I guess.

ROSE: And it doesn't have to be a business of a questionable nature. He'll set you up in an honest one.

RAY: Not as much money in honest business, Rose.

ROSE: Yeah, but that's what it'll be. This questionable shit is just temporary. Until we can get back on our feet again. As soon as we do, we go legit. We won't desecrate your mother's memory by continuing to earn our daily bread in a questionable manner one minute longer than we absolutely have to. I won't stand for anything else. And neither will your father.

RAY: Dad don't stand for anything. He don't stand at all. He just falls down all the time.

BILLY: That's not fair, Ray. You'd fall down too if you drank as much as he does.

RAY: Hey, you wanna be fair, let's be fair. Truth is, he don't fall down at all no more—you can't fall down if you don't ever get up off your ass in the first place.

ROSE: Alright, that's enough. We'll have no more talk of that kind around here. You have some respect for your father. He brought you into the world.

BILLY: I shouldn't thank him for that, Rose. I should kick him in the teeth for it.

ROSE: That's enough of that, Billy. I don't wanna hear it.

RAY: Cut it out, Billy.

BILLY: You started it.

RAY: Okay, and I'm ending it too, alright?

BILLY: Yeah, fine—jeeze—Louise…

(Beat)

CURTIS: *(Offstage:)* WHERE'S MY FORTIFICATION!?!

(Beat. ROSE *gets up and goes to a cabinet. She hesitates. Then she takes out another, unopened bottle of whiskey, and exits.)*

BILLY: He's a bastard.

RAY: I know.

CURTIS: DOES ANYONE MIND TELLING ME WERE MY FORTIFICATION HAS BEEN STASHED?

BILLY: She should be in college.

RAY: I know.

CURTIS: OR IS IT TOO MUCH TROUBLE TO ALLOW AN OLD MAN TO INDULGE IN A LITTLE FORTIFICATION NOW AND THEN?

BILLY: She shouldn't be here at all.

RAY: I know.

CURTIS: GOD KNOWS, I DON'T EXPECT ANY DECENT FORTIFICATION!

RAY: Times are tough.

CURTIS: BUT IS IT TOO MUCH TO EVEN ALLOW ME THE CRAPPY STUFF?

BILLY: I hate him.

RAY: Don't say that.

CURTIS: MAYBE WE CAN JUST BUY THE GENERIC KIND! CAN WE AFFORD THAT?

BILLY: I do.

RAY: I know. *(Beat)* He got his fortification.

BILLY: I'm gonna bring him motor oil one day.

RAY: He won't notice the difference.

(Beat)

BILLY: It ain't fair. When you and me got old enough to work and care for ourselves, Rose shoulda gone to to college. She had the grades. They were gonna give her a free ride.

RAY: I know it.

BILLY: But that fucking bastard.

RAY: I know it.

BILLY: That fucking bastard pretended to be even more sick than he was when mom died so she'd stay here and take are of him, the fucking prick.

RAY: I know it.

(Beat)

BILLY: I should go to college.

RAY: What would you major in? Fucking-Up Studies? You're not smart enough to college.

BILLY: The Big Bossman thinks I'm smart enough.

RAY: Only 'cause you keep your mouth shut around him. He thinks you're thinking deep thoughts all the time. You put more than two words together, he'll figure out the reality of the situation soon enough.

(Beat)

BILLY: You ain't much for a fella's self-esteem, you know that?

(Beat)

RAY: That's why this job is so important, Billy. If we can make enough money, Rose can go back to college. We can move out of this pit and get a decent home. Maybe we can ship the old man off to some kinda home for decrepit drunks, or something. There's real opportunities in this line of business, Billy. You just gotta stay outta trouble and do right by the Boss.

BILLY: Rose won't let us ship the old coot off to no home.

RAY: We'll work somethin' out. Get a nurse or somethin'.

BILLY: A nurse costs money.

RAY: We'll have money.

BILLY: Yeah. Right. I forgot that was part of this particular scenario.

RAY: This is, like…I don't know if you can even remember Ma, when we was really little…

BILLY: I remember her when we was bigger.

RAY: When we was little, Billy, I'm telling you…your Mom, she was like…she was like the hottest thing in the neighborhood.

BILLY: Yeah?

RAY: Yeah. Like, I remember being so proud, 'cause my Mom was so much better looking than the moms of all my friends, you know. She was pretty, and she was… well, it didn't…I mean, yeah, sure, my old man was fucking drunk, but who cared, 'cause of Mom… *(Beat)* So, that old fuck in there wore her down and by the time she died, she looked like an old hag.

BILLY: She did not.

RAY: Yeah, she did. Compared to how she looked when we was little, she looked like an old hag. She was twenty years older than how old she really was, in the way she looked. Christ. I never even knew how fucking poor we were until after she died, 'cause she did such a good job of making sure we always had everything we needed. She wanted things for us, Billy. Good things. Better things. And I see the same thing happening to Rose that happened to Mom, I see her getting worn down and haggard and not pretty anymore and looking older than she really is. You remember how pretty Rose used to be?

BILLY: She's still pretty.

RAY: Not as pretty as how she used to be. And a year from now, she'll be less pretty than she is today. I'm not gonna let that happen to her, Billy. *(Beat)* I see the news, Billy, I read the headlines, and yeah, times are tough, but not for everyone, Billy, there are all these people out there, all these no-talent people, getting all those things that Mom wanted for us, not for them, for us, but they're getting those things, not us, they're making money hand over fist, buying all these things, living in these…*houses*, driving these…*cars*, wearing these…*clothes*. I'm talking about morons, geeks, I mean, C E Os, Pop Stars, Porn Stars, Reality T V Stars, Hedge Fund Fuckers, Wall Street Traders, all these people are so fucking richer than we are, Billy, so fucking unworthy of it, and I'm fucking sick of it. I'm fucking sick of being fucking last on Santa's fucking list, you know what I mean, like a fucking afterthought. I'm sick of waiting, and I'm gonna fucking grab this opportunity while I can, grab it by the fucking balls, I'm going to make something for myself and for this family or I'm going to choke on my own vomit.

(Beat)

BILLY: Gross.

(Beat)

RAY: Billy?

BILLY: Yeah?

RAY: Don't blow it, O K?

BILLY: Yeah. Right. O K. *(Beat)* What does she mean, "Elvis has left the building?"

(Beat)

(End of Scene)

Scene Three

(Home)

(A few days later)

ROSE: What do you mean, he just took off?

RAY: I mean he just took off. I turned around and he wasn't there. One minute he was, the next minute he wasn't. He just left. He didn't tell me where he was goin' or nothin'. He just took off.

ROSE: Well, where'd he go?

RAY: I don't know! We were done for the day. It was time to go home. And he just took off.

ROSE: Well, did you see him running across the street to the ice cream truck or something?

RAY: I didn't see him at all.

ROSE: Was the ice cream truck in the vicinity?

RAY: There was no ice cream truck.

ROSE: Are you sure? Did you hear the little rinky-dink song? *(She hums "Pop Goes the Weasel":)*Dah-dah dah-dah, dah-da-de-de-dah, dah-dah dah-dah dah-dee-da—

RAY: I know what the fucking song is, Rose!

ROSE: Don't get pissy with me! You're the one who lost your brother!

RAY: I didn't lose him! He just took off! He went AWOL!

ROSE: Did he have any money?

RAY: A little. Not enough to go very far. Why, you think he got on a bus?

ROSE: He probably did get on a bus. I just hope it was a city bus, and not a Greyhound.

RAY: Why would he get on a Greyhound, Rose?

ROSE: Why does your brother do half the things he does?

RAY: Ah, jeeze—

ROSE: I'm very worried about this, Ray.

RAY: So am I.

ROSE: Why'd he run off like that? Was he upset?

RAY: NO! Everything was great. He was doing his job and he wasn't complaining. The Bossman liked the work we was doing. He said we were efficient and discreet. Everything was fine.

ROSE: Then what's he up to?

RAY: I don't know! Prob'ly nothin'. Prob'ly he's gone to see a flick or somethin'.

ROSE: I don't know. I get nervous when Billy goes out alone.

BILLY: I know. He's such a fuckin' retard.

ROSE: Don't say that. He's not a retard. Not clinically.

RAY: He's not a mongoloid or nothin', but he's a retard. He probably had fetal alcohol syndrome or something.

ROSE: You get that from the mother, not from the father.

RAY: Well, he's still a retard, Rose, there's no way around it. You ever looked inside his eyes, like, really hard? Nothing there, Rose. Out to fuckin' lunch.

ROSE: Don't say that about your brother.

(Beat. The front door opens, and BILLY *enters, a plastic bag in his hands. He is followed by* VIOLET. *She is dressed in such a way as to immediately identify herself as a prostitute.*

Long pause, as BILLY *stands there smiling,* VIOLET *looks around nervously, and* RAY *and* ROSE *stare wide eyed, in horror.)*

RAY: Who's this, Billy?

ROSE: What have you got here, Billy?

BILLY: I got us some D V Ds. Five D V Ds. Five movies on D V D. Actually, three on D V D, two on Blu-ray. All here in this bag. Things are looking up around here, I'm telling you. We have arrived.

(Beat)

RAY: We haven't got a D V D player, Billy. Or a Blu-ray.

BILLY: Yeah. Well, that's cool. I'll buy us one. A brand new, state of the art D V D/Blu-ray player.

RAY: Yeah? With what money?

BILLY: We're making money.

ROSE: I've got your money. That money goes to the household, not to home entertainment.

BILLY: Home entertainment is a legitimate household expense.

ROSE: Rent is a more legitimate household expense.

BILLY: Fine. Then I'll put it on the card.

RAY: Card?

BILLY: My American Express Card, Ray.

RAY: You don't have an American Express Card, Billy.

BILLY: I do now, Ray. Membership has its fucking privileges.

RAY: Where'd you get that card, Billy?

BILLY: Don't worry about it.

RAY: Where'd you get it?

BILLY: From this guy.

RAY: WHAT GUY?

BILLY: This guy.

RAY: WHAT GUY?

BILLY: Just some guy.

RAY: Did…did you get it from her…John?

VIOLET: *(She has an accent.)* "Client".

RAY: What?

VIOLET: "Client". We call them "clients".

RAY: What are you, some kinda attorney?

VIOLET: I've never been compared to an attorney, no, but sometimes I've heard an attorney compared to me.

RAY: What, you're all hoidy and toidy, you don't got Johns, you got clients, I guess you don't suck cock either, you perform acts of oral pleasure.

ROSE: Ray! Language!

VIOLET: Hey, fuck you buddy, I don't know what makes you such a hard ass, the Pope bless your testicles or something? What are you, Mother Teresa? The Flying Nun? Something about you makes you more moral than me 'cause you don't do it for money, you just pay to do it?

RAY: Hey, I never paid no one to do nothing.

VIOLET: We all pay, Sister Mary Sunshine, one way or another.

RAY: I'm not talking to you. I'm talking to him. *(To* BILLY*:)* Billy: You got that American Express Card from her…"client"?

(Beat)

BILLY: Yes.

(RAY slaps BILLY across his face, very hard.)

BILLY: Christ, you're always hittin' me! That's all you ever do is hit me! I think that's what you live for! You live for smackin' me in the face!

RAY: *(Grabbing BILLY by his collar:)* You're an idiot, Billy!

BILLY: So what! That's not a crime, is it?!?

RAY: Where'd she come from, Billy? Tell me. Where'd she come from?

BILLY: I dunno! Nebraska! New Jersey! Seattle! I dunno! Ask her!

VIOLET: Vladivostok, originally.

BILLY: Vladi—what she said. Originally.

RAY: Is she one of the Big Bossman's ladies? Is she? *(Beat)* Is she?

BILLY: You're gonna hit me again!

RAY: Is she?

(Beat)

BILLY: Yeah.

(RAY hits BILLY again.)

BILLY: I knew you were gonna do that! I knew you were! That's all you ever do! That's all I ever get around here!

RAY: What is she doing here, Billy? Tell me that. What is she doing here?

(Beat)

BILLY: I assisted her.

RAY: You what?

BILLY: I assisted her.

RAY: In what?

BILLY: In leaving.

(Beat. RAY *is stunned. He lets go of* BILLY, *walks away, and sits at the table with his head in his hands. Beat)*

ROSE: Have a seat Miss…?

VIOLET: Call me Violet.

ROSE: *(Beat)* O K. Won't you have a seat?

VIOLET: Don't mind if I do.

(Beat)

BILLY: Aren't you gonna hit me, Ray? C'mon, hit me. It's O K. I won't complain. Hit me. I deserve it. Come on. *(Beat)* Don't be mad, Ray. Don't be angry. Lookit all the movies I brought home. I brought home great movies. Look what I got. *(He starts taking movies out of the bag, one by one.)* I got: *The Alamo*, with John Wayne and Richard Widmark. Only movie John Wayne ever directed, Ray, did ya' know that? Pretty historical, huh? Look what else I got. I got: *The French Connection*, that's one a' your favorites, innit? That's the one with the big car chase, right? I love that car chase. Best movie car chase of all time. Without a doubt. Bar none. Except maybe for the one in *Bullett*. With Steve McQueen. They were outta that one, Ray. But, look what else I got. I got: *Casablanca*. That's a classic, Ray, it really is a true classic. Bogart's in it. I love Bogart. He's the greatest. Definitely. Bar none. Except maybe Steve McQueen. Look. I got: *Moby Dick*. Greg Peck's in that one. That's the one about the whale. The big one. The big white one. The big white whale that eats ships and people and stuff. Greg Peck's the captain with the big scar through his face and only one leg. You know the one, Ray. We saw it on T V when we was kids. You remember. Greg Peck on toppa that whale, stabbin' it with a harpoon? You 'member? Doncha? Doncha, Ray? Huh? Ray? Doncha?

(Beat)

ROSE: We can't play those movies, Billy.

BILLY: That don't matter. We'll use our imaginations. We've seen all these movies before. We'll act 'em out. If we forget what happens next, we'll just make it up. It'll be fun.

VIOLET: Was *The Alamo* really the only movie John Wayne ever directed?

BILLY: Only one.

VIOLET: I thought there was another.

BILLY: Nope.

VIOLET: I think maybe there was another, yeah.

BILLY: *The Alamo.* 1960-ish. Only one.

VIOLET: I'm not totally sure about that.

RAY: We've got to bring her back.

VIOLET: Bring who back?

BILLY: Back where?

RAY: To the Big Bossman.

VIOLET: Who're we talkin' about, here?

BILLY: We can't do that, Ray.

RAY: We have to.

VIOLET: We don't have to do nothin' we don't want to. This here is a free country, right?

BILLY: We can't, Ray.

VIOLET: I don't wanna go back.

BILLY: She don't wanna go back.

RAY: That's not our problem.

BILLY: It's mine. The Big Bossman wouldn't let her go. She wanted to go. I assisted her in going.

RAY: Why the fuck did you do that, Billy?

BILLY: It was the nice thing to do, Ray.

VIOLET: He's right about that. It was very nice.

ROSE: Can I offer you something? Tea, or something? Miss…Violet?

VIOLET: Oh, yes, thank you, that would be very nice. I like tea. Earl Grey, if you got it. With milk.

ROSE: Darjeeling?

VIOLET: Hey, whatever. Beggars and choosers, don't ya' know.

RAY: It's fine to be nice, Billy. But why do you want to be *that* fuckin' nice?

BILLY: I don't want to be. The situation called for it.

RAY: Couldn't you have just helped an old lady cross the fucking street, you wanna be nice?

ROSE: *(Pouring tea:)* This was, on the scale of things, not high on the list of smart moves, Billy. Of which you haven't made a lot to begin with. No offense to you, Violet.

VIOLET: Whatever.

BILLY: I was just being nice.

RAY: Not very nice to the Bossman though, is it? Taking one of his ladies without permission.

VIOLET: Yeah, hey, well, he was keeping me from leaving without my permission.

RAY: What about the Big Bossman, Billy?

BILLY: What about him?

RAY: What about his rights?

VIOLET: What rights?

RAY: His property rights.

VIOLET: I look like a Honda Civic to you?

RAY: What?

VIOLET: I look like a Honda Civic or a Pontiac or an i-Pod or a diamond tiara?

ROSE: You don't look like any of those things.

VIOLET: I look like a thing, or I look like a person, here?

BILLY: A person. You definitely look like a person.

VIOLET: That's right. I'm a person. I look like a thing you own? An object? A piece of property?

BILLY: You look like a person.

VIOLET: Well, last I checked, it said you couldn't own a person like a piece of property. I think you took care of that one with the Declaration of Independence.

ROSE: The Emancipation Proclamation.

VIOLET: Emancipation Declaration.

ROSE: And the 13th Amendment.

VIOLET: Your 13th Emancipated Proclaimed Declaration of Amendment.

(Beat)

RAY: You're not a citizen.

BILLY: That don't matter, Ray.

RAY: You can't own a person. But you can contract them for their labor or their…kidneys, or whatever. They don't fulfill their end of the contract, you can get an injunction. An injunction to prevent them from going back to Vladivostok until they've fulfilled their labor contract with the Bossman.

VIOLET: I can't go back to Vladivostok because the Big Bossman took my passport.

RAY: It's called free enterprise, lady.

VIOLET: Well, fuck you, Alan Greenspan, and kiss my ass.

ROSE: You're going to get in a bucket of trouble, Billy.

BILLY: I can take it.

ROSE: No, you can't. Don't make out like a hard guy, Billy. You're not a hard guy. Just a fuckin' dumbass kid, with a mild case of developmental disability.

RAY: See! I told you he was a fuckin' retard!

BILLY: I'm not a retard!

VIOLET: 'Course you're not.

BILLY: Thanks.

VIOLET: No prob.

BILLY: Violet don't think I'm a retard.

RAY: Do you know what this means? Do you? Have you got the slightest idea of what this means? We could get wasted for this, you big blockhead! As in, we could wake up DEAD over this fuckin' whore!

VIOLET: Excuse me. I am in the room here.

RAY: Are you fucking her, Billy?

BILLY: What?

RAY: Are you fucking her?

BILLY: No!

RAY: You're not fucking her?

VIOLET: Excuse me, but I haven't gone anywhere since announcing my presence here in the room just moments previously to now. I am still here, sitting right here, in case anybody was wondering, and I ain't deaf or nothing like that, in case that was what you were thinking, here.

RAY: Are you *trying* to fuck her, then? Is that what this is about? Like, some kind of courtship ritual?

BILLY: No!

RAY: Don't lie to me.

BILLY: I'm not like that!

VIOLET: He's not, either.

RAY: You think she'll fuck you if you help her?

VIOLET: Hello!

RAY: *(To* VIOLET:*)* Will you fuck him?

VIOLET: Excuse me?

RAY: Will you fuck him? Will you fuck him for helping you out? Come on, tell him. Let's get it out in the open.

VIOLET: Who I fuck and for what reasons I fuck them is none of your fucking business, mister.

RAY: It's the Big Bossman's business.

VIOLET: Not no more, it isn't.

RAY: It's my business, too, because this is my brother we're talking about here, my retard brother.

BILLY: I'm not a retard.

RAY: I want to know if you're planning on fucking my retard brother, here! Or performing and act of oral pleasure on him!

VIOLET: You're hostile.

RAY: Whore!

VIOLET: Asshole!

RAY: Cunt!

VIOLET: Bitch!

RAY: Whore!

VIOLET: You said that one, already.

ROSE: O K, that's enough, Ray.

RAY: I'm trying to establish some facts, here.

ROSE: Enough.

(Beat)

RAY: Whatever.

ROSE: Why'd you have to bring her here, Billy?

VIOLET: People can talk about me like I'm actually in the room, you know. People either pretend I'm not here, or they talk to me like I'm worse than the gum stuck to the bottom of their shoe.

BILLY: Where else could I bring her? She wanted to leave. And she couldn't. What was I gonna do?

(Beat)

VIOLET: You know, it's really not as bad as it seems. I mean, I can pull my own weight, y'know. I can cook and do laundry. Hell, I can even type. I could get a job as a secretary. Workin' for some big executive type. I'll bring in tons of money. At least fifteen dollars an hour. Maybe twenty. *(Beat)* O K. Look. I'll turn tricks again if I have to. I don't want to, but I will if I have to, O K? But not for the Big Bossman. O K?

(Beat. Everyone looks at her.)

ROSE: That won't be necessary, Violet.

VIOLET: Well, I mean, I'm not helpless, y'know. I'm a pretty independent person. I just happen to be a little down on my luck right now, and I could use a helping hand. *(Beat. She stands, and walks into the middle of the room. Beat. She disrobes. She stands, there, naked. In addition to some conspicuous bruises, her body is marked with black ink into sections. She turns slowly in a circle, so everyone in the room can see.)* This is what he said he's do to me. Cut me up. Like this. Into pieces. Into sections. Like you'd do with a cow. Or a chicken. This is what he said he'd do to me if I left. I don't know what kind of ink he used. I can't seem to scrub it off. I think it was a Sharpie. *(Beat. She points to a mark on her buttock.)* Can't scrub this off, either. This is permanent. He gave

this to me. Burned it into my flesh. When I first came
to work for him. *(She points to another scar on her chest.)*
This one too. His brand, he calls it. He really has an
actual branding iron he had specially made for the
purpose. Like he's John Fucking Wayne in *Red* Fucking
River. Branding cattle. "B.B." For Big Bossman. He says
it's so everyone knows who his ladies belong to. And
if anyone ever tries to pimp one of us out behind his
back, they can't claim they didn't know what they was
doing. *(Beat)* He's such a smooth operator. I'd already
been a whore in Dubai. I was just sixteen. He bought
me. He acted all helpful. Bought me breakfast. Acted
so concerned. Comes off so worldly, and so concerned
at the same time. Like Sebastian Fucking Cabot. Said
we could do business together. Said he wouldn't be
like the others. Me, just sixteen. I figured working for
him couldn't be worse than working in Dubai. *(Beat)*
I'm one of the oldest girls working for him, now. Most
don't make it as long as me. We lose our looks. Or
we die. *(Beat)* Look, I'm sorry to impose on you good
people. I really am. It's not my way to impose upon
anybody, for anything. This is not something I do on
a regular basis or anything. It's not something I enjoy
doing. It's not something I'm enjoying now, delightful
people though you are. I mean, I know this must be
a terrible inconvenience to you all. Here you are at
home, just trying to get on with your life, and in walks
trouble. Someone who could get you in trouble. Who
could get you in trouble with your boss. With THE
Boss. I know, it's not a nice position to be put in. And
I'm sorry to put you in it. Really, I am. And I wouldn't
blame you at all if you were to ask me to leave. I
wouldn't resent it a bit. I'd understand completely.
I mean, you're under no obligation to help me. No
obligation at all. That's the bottom line. You do not
have to help me out. *(Beat)* But I'm asking you to.

(Beat. Everyone looks at VIOLET, *not knowing what to say.)*

(A knock at the door)

(Beat. Everyone stands frozen, fearful.)

(Another knock at the door. Everyone looks around. Another knock. The knocking is polite, but insistent. ROSE *finally goes to answer the door. It is the* BIG BOSSMAN, *hat in hand. He is big, although it is as much muscle as fat. He is incredibly polite, well spoken, and formal. Rose makes sure he can't see the others inside.)*

BIG BOSSMAN: Evening, Ma'am. Pardon my intrusion, but is this the domicile of Billy and Ray?

ROSE: Yes, it is, sir.

BIG BOSSMAN: Perchance, are Billy or Ray in, Ma'am?

ROSE: Uhh, no. Perchance they are not.

BIG BOSSMAN: Ah, I see. That is confoundedly unfortunate. My business with them is of a highly importunate nature, you see.

ROSE: I see.

BIG BOSSMAN: Might I trouble you to allow me to wait for them in your living room or kitchen? I promise you I shall remain as quiet as possible, and as out of the way as my girth permits me.

ROSE: I'm sorry sir, but I never let strangers into the apartment.

BIG BOSSMAN: Of course, of course. However, I am not a stranger, Ma'am. I am Billy and Ray's employer.

ROSE: Be that as it may sir, I cannot let you into my home as I have never met you before tonight. And while you seem like a perfectly trustworthy and reputable individual, well, looks can be deceiving, can't they?

BIG BOSSMAN: Of course. I quite understand. If you would be so kind, Ma'am, when do you expect Billy and Ray to return?

ROSE: I don't know, sir. You see, they've left town.

BIG BOSSMAN: Have they? Oh. That is unfortunate.

ROSE: And most unexpected.

BIG BOSSMAN: I see.

ROSE: And most sudden.

BIG BOSSMAN: Oh my.

ROSE: Yes indeed, sir.

BIG BOSSMAN: Can you tell me where they have gone?

ROSE: I would if I could, but I can't. They left no forwarding address.

BIG BOSSMAN: Oh my. I certainly hope nothing of an ill nature has befallen them.

ROSE: We can only pray, sir. We can only pray.

BIG BOSSMAN: Yes, well. I'll leave the prayers to you.

ROSE: I thank you for your concern.

BIG BOSSMAN: Any time, Ma'am. Any time. Good evening.

ROSE: And a good evening to you, sir.

(ROSE *shuts the door. Everyone is silent. Suddenly, the door slams open.* FRANCIS *stands in the doorway. He is an imposing, powerful-looking man.*)

FRANCIS: The door. It swunged itself open of its own accordance.

(FRANCIS *enters, followed by* BIG BOSSMAN. BIG BOSSMAN *sees* BILLY, RAY *and* VIOLET.)

BIG BOSSMAN: Hello, Billy. I thought you were out of town.

FRANCIS: The Bossman thought that through the fleetness of your feet you had vacated the vicinity of the metropolis.

BILLY: Just got back sir. What brings you to this neck of the woods?

BIG BOSSMAN: Business, Billy.

FRANCIS: The Bossman has been brought to your abode in this section of the timberland by the necessity of conducting matters of a commercial natural.

BIG BOSSMAN: A very serious business concern. Hello, Ray.

RAY: Hello, Boss.

BIG BOSSMAN: Hello, Violet.

VIOLET: Hiya, Boss.

BIG BOSSMAN: You're making a rather immodest spectacle of yourself this evening.

FRANCIS: The Big Bossman wonders why it is you are appearing in such a state of bare-assedness at this present time.

(VIOLET *starts to get dressed.*)

BIG BOSSMAN: Did I tell you to get dressed?

(*Beat.* VIOLET *stops getting dressed.*)

BIG BOSSMAN: What are those marks on your torso?

FRANCIS: The Big Bossman inquires as to the nature of the drawings upon your cadaver.

VIOLET: You drew 'em, Boss.

(*Long pause*)

BIG BOSSMAN: Did I? (*Beat*) I believe everyone here knows Francis.

BILLY: 'Cept Rose.

BIG BOSSMAN: Ah, yes. Ray?

RAY: Yes, Boss?

BIG BOSSMAN: Aren't you going to introduce me to our hostess?

RAY: Uh, yes, of course. Boss, I'd like you to meet our sister, Rose.

BIG BOSSMAN: *(Graciously taking her hand and bowing slightly:)* A beautiful name for a beautiful flower and a beautiful woman. A pleasure, Ma'am, a genuine pleasure. Billy and Ray speak most highly of you, and I can see that they do not exaggerate.

ROSE: Uh, yeah. Thanks.

BIG BOSSMAN: And this gentleman is my trusted aide, Francis.

ROSE: O K.

BIG BOSSMAN: *(He sits at the kitchen table, and hands his hat and cane to* FRANCIS, *who stands behind him.)* Violet. For heaven's sake. Put some clothes on.

FRANCIS: The Big Bossman respectfully requests that you cover your nakedness with decorous garmentation and re-clothe your dishabillated carcass.

(Beat. Then, VIOLET *gets dressed.* BILLY *shifts around anxiously, while* RAY *remains still and at a distance.)*

(Suddenly, ROSE *takes a seat by* BIG BOSSMAN.*)*

ROSE: And Francis…?

BIG BOSSMAN: Francis is already dressed.

FRANCIS: Francis is currently in a state of dressedness that cloaks his au-naturality.

ROSE: But would he like a seat?

BIG BOSSMAN: Francis prefers to stand.

FRANCIS: Francis prefers to predominate in a position whereby his feet remain planted and his torso remains perpendicular.

ROSE: I see. Tell me, then, sir, if I might… How's business?

BIG BOSSMAN: On the whole, business is good, Miss Rose. There are, however, one or two…or three small problems that need to be ironed out. Which is what brings me here, seeking the advice of your two able brothers.

ROSE: Oh, my brothers don't know the first thing about business, sir.

BIG BOSSMAN: I think they know quite a bit more than you would expect, Miss Rose.

ROSE: Oh, I'm kinda doubtful about that. They've never made one red cent themselves, not in all their whole lives long.

BIG BOSSMAN: Surely you exaggerate, Miss Rose.

ROSE: I only wish I did. This is not a family of money-makers, that's the sad truth of the matter. This is a family of just-barely survivors. We're the kind of family that is always just to one side of complete and total horrible devastation. We come from ignorant immigrants, whose hard work didn't get them terribly far into the middle class, and recent developments have drawn us considerably south of the less desirable side of that demarcation. We're the kind of folks whose fathers worked in the factories and whose sons work in McDonald's.

BILLY: Except Dad never worked in nothing at all.

RAY: Shut up!

BIG BOSSMAN: Your situation was about to change. There is no family so poor that it may not rise above its station, Miss Rose. Our new president is surely proof of that, is he not? A man named Barack Hussein Obama is not destined to rule the free world unless it is he himself who wills it. As we all will our own destinies—as I have willed my own. I was not to manor born, Miss Rose. I hail from circumstances not unlike your own. But I am an entrepreneur. That is a natural talent, Miss Rose. It is not something that is either learned or inherited. I have a keen and unusual talent for recognizing the needs of a community that are not being met, and setting up enterprises to meet them.

BILLY: Can we cut the crap here?

ROSE: Shut up, Billy.

RAY: Shut up, Billy.

VIOLET: Shut up, Billy.

BIG BOSSMAN: Billy, you are extremely rude to a very gracious woman.

FRANCIS: The rudenosity of the one known as William is indubitably disappreciated.

BIG BOSSMAN: Nevertheless, Miss Rose, Billy does have a point. Your brothers and I do have some sensitive information to discuss. So if you will be so kind as to excuse us…?

ROSE: Go right ahead.

(Beat)

BIG BOSSMAN: Would you like us to adjoin to another room?

ROSE: You can stay right here. You'll be more comfortable. There's more space.

(Beat)

BIG BOSSMAN: Then if you'll excuse us…?

ROSE: Of course. You're excused.

(Beat)

BIG BOSSMAN: Pardon me, but just when will you excuse us?

ROSE: You're already excused, sir.

BIG BOSSMAN: I see. I fear that I have failed to make myself clear. Miss Rose: Please forgive my old fashioned sense of decorum, but it is a policy of mine never to discuss business in the presence of a Lady.

ROSE: That's a very old-fashioned policy, sir.

BIG BOSSMAN: Not in my business, Miss Rose.

ROSE: But what about Violet?

BIG BOSSMAN: Violet, Miss Rose, is not a lady.

VIOLET: Hello! Right here!

BIG BOSSMAN: I must be frank, Miss Rose: If you would be so kind as to leave the room for the duration of the business that Ray and Billy and I have together, I should be most grateful.

ROSE: Forgive me, sir, but there is not a word spoken in this house that cannot fall upon these ears.

BIG BOSSMAN: Then, perhaps I had better take our business elsewhere.

ROSE: Not now. I cannot allow Billy and Ray out in this nasty weather. They might catch cold.

(Beat)

BIG BOSSMAN: It's actually quite mild, tonight.

ROSE: Even so. These things can change. *(She snaps her fingers:)* Just like that.

(Beat)

BIG BOSSMAN: You seem quite protective of your brothers.

ROSE: Well, you see, sir. I raised them. After our mother died. We were just kids. But was two years older than Ray, so I became the parent. I cooked, cleaned, and cared for them, and for our ailing father. I filled out the applications for Food Stamps and public assistance, forged our father's signature, and put them in the mail. I did all the things a parent is supposed to do. So, naturally, I am somewhat parentally protective of them.

BIG BOSSMAN: That's very touching. You are a woman of tremendous character and fortitude.

ROSE: Hardly.

BIG BOSSMAN: I shall, of course, respect your wishes, Miss Rose. I shall ask you once more— Will you, please, as a favor to me, leave the room?

ROSE: Sorry, sir. I will not.

(Beat)

BIG BOSSMAN: Very well. As you wish. *(He stands, with his walking stick.)* You have something of mine, Gentlemen.

BILLY: What's that, Boss?

RAY: Billy…

BIG BOSSMAN: I think you know what that is, Billy.

BILLY: Why don't you tell me, Boss?

RAY: Billy…

BIG BOSSMAN: Don't play dumb, Billy. I know you're not dumb.

BILLY: I am, Boss. I'm very dumb. I'm a really dumb guy. I am. I can't even tie my own shoes, I'm so dumb. I don't know my own name, I'm so dumb. I'm really, really dumb. That's what everyone's always telling me.

BIG BOSSMAN: You play dumb, Billy, but you're not. I can see the wheels turning behind your eyes.

BILLY: That's usually 'cause I'm, like, trying to figure out which side is my right and which is my left, Boss.

BIG BOSSMAN: You have something of mine, Billy.

BILLY: What's that, Boss?

BIG BOSSMAN: A girl named Violet.

BILLY: What about her?

RAY: Billy…

BIG BOSSMAN: She works for me.

BILLY: So?

RAY: Billy…

BIG BOSSMAN: And she's over here.

BILLY: Yeah?

BIG BOSSMAN: And she's not supposed to be.

BILLY: I see.

BIG BOSSMAN: And I want her back where she's supposed to be.

BILLY: You do?

BIG BOSSMAN: Yes.

BILLY: Oh.

BIG BOSSMAN: Do I make myself clear?

BILLY: Perfectly frank.

RAY: Godamnit, Billy…!

BIG BOSSMAN: I think you're a bright boy, Billy. Even though you do everything on earth that you can to prove me wrong. Do you even know what you've done? Do you have any idea? You have created a situation that could cause me terrific embarrassment. If I hadn't rushed over here at my own time and expense, things could have gotten dangerously out of hand. I might easily have been forced to commit an act of...*unpleasantness* in order to remedy this situation. This is a very complicated business we are in, boys, and appearances count. They count quite a bit. And to make things all the worse, you've implicated your brother in this as well. That's not a very considerate position to put a brother in.

BILLY: Sorry, Ray.

BIG BOSSMAN: Now, I'm willing to overlook this little episode. I have a bruised and angry customer who wants his American Express Card back, but he's from out of town, and I don't think he's going to be a significant problem. I'm putting myself out on the line, boys, but I'm willing to do that for you. I have a great deal of faith in you both. I think you have... possibilities. I think you could both be very valuable to me. Provided you have learned your lesson. And I think that you have.

RAY: We have, Boss, we certainly have.

BIG BOSSMAN: Good. I'm glad to hear it. Now, if you will be so good as to turn over the lady in question, we can all go home and go to bed.

BILLY: There's a problem with that, Boss.

RAY: Shut up, Billy!

BIG BOSSMAN: Problem?

BILLY: Yes.

BIG BOSSMAN: What problem?

RAY: Just stop talkin', Billy!

BILLY: She don't wanna go with you.

BIG BOSSMAN: (*Looking directly at* BILLY) What has that got to do with anything, Billy?

BILLY: Well, now, I'm not exactly an expert when it comes to this stuff, y'know, but I guess what I'm gettin' at here is that it sorta has got everything to do with everything, Boss. *(Beat)* You're not takin' her anywhere she don't wanna go, Boss.

RAY: Goddamnit!

BIG BOSSMAN: Good heavens. Billy, you're not asking me to believe you are doing this for Violet's benefit?

BILLY: I'm not asking you to believe anything.

BIG BOSSMAN: Billy, Billy, Billy. I know…Francis knows…everyone knows, I suspect even Violet knows, that the only reason you are doing this is to set yourself up as Violet's pimp.

VIOLET: Is that why you are doing this, Billy?

BILLY: No, of course not.

BIG BOSSMAN: You're a liar, Billy. The only question is if you are also lying to yourself.

BILLY: Yeah. Well go take a flying fuck.

(Beat)

RAY: Oh, shit.

BIG BOSSMAN: Miss Rose, I really must insist that you leave the room now.

FRANCIS: The Bossman respectfully requests the absence of your presence at this precise moment in time.

ROSE: No can do.

(Beat)

BIG BOSSMAN: Very well. *(Beat)* Did I ever tell you boys how I became the man I am? How I got my start in business? I'll tell you. It was some time ago. I was a young sprout, younger than yourselves, and I was impetuous, and reckless, and I was in debt. I owned

money I could not pay. And I received an ultimatum:
Pay up, or my fingers would be broken. Now, I had
never had my fingers broken before, but I had seen it
done, and it very much looked to me like it hurt. A lot.
Terribly. And the fingers, I was wise enough to know,
although at this time in my life I was not wise about
much, were only the beginning. First fingers, then
arms, then kneecaps. By the end, I would be crippled,
a culmination devoutly to be avoided, figured I. But I
had nothing. Not a damn thing. No cash, and nothing
to sell…no stereo, no car, no narcotics, no nothing.
(Beat) Except one thing. *(Beat)* I had Miranda. *(Beat)*
Miranda was my girl, you see, my sweetheart. She was
the most beautiful girl I ever did see, and that opinion
was shared by everyone in the neighborhood. Black
curls cascading down her long neck. Lips, round and
full. Long arms, legs up to here, breasts and buttocks
firm and true, and thighs that would not quit. I loved
her. God, how I loved her. And she, for some reason,
loved me. *(Beat)* This was a calamitous mistake. *(Beat)*
She loved me fiercely. She would have done anything
for me. Anything at all. *(Beat)* And so she did. *(Beat)*
I asked Miranda, who loved me, to help me out. To
save me from almost certain crippledom, and very
likely, ultimately, death. And, although she did not
want to, although it hurt her terribly to do so, hurt
here where it counted…in her heart…despite that, she
sacrificed herself, sacrificed her virtue, for me. *(Beat)*
And I paid my debtors in trade. *(Beat)* I paid them with
Miranda. *(Beat)* But that was not the end. You might
have thought that was the end, but it was not…but
of course, you knew that was not the end, for had it
been, what would I be doing here now? No, the sexual
favors Miranda performed to bail me out of debt were
not the last she would perform, because I had realized
something. I realized, I had an asset. I had something
that was worth something, that people wanted, that

they would pay for. I had Miranda. *(Beat)* Who began to turn tricks for me. *(Beat)* And soon we had money. And soon I had several more girls hooking for me. And all, for a time, was well with the world. *(Beat)* But not so with Miranda. *(Beat)* Who left me, both professionally and personally. For another guy. For another pimp. *(Beat)* Who could blame her? *(Beat)* I did not. *(Beat)* But that did not mean I could just let her go. *(Beat)* Because by this time, I was a businessman. I was a businessman, with a thriving business, and a reputation to uphold. And reputations are important, in the business world, in this line of work, especially. As I mentioned, appearances do count. They count quite a bit. *(Beat)* So, I hunted her down. *(Beat)* And when I found her, I cut off her boyfriend's testicles and I fed them to him, while Miranda watched. *(Beat)* And then I cut her face, several times, deep, and hard, so it would scar, and she could never turn tricks for anyone, ever again. *(Beat)* And in this way, I gained a reputation, which was, shall we say, formidable. *(Beat)* A reputation, I might add, I have managed to maintain. *(Beat)* Sometimes with deeds even more atrocious. *(Beat)* And remember this: I loved her. This is not hyperbole. I truly did. I loved Miranda, dearly, more than anything I have ever loved before or since. And still, I did this to her. Even though I loved her. *(Beat. To* BILLY, RAY, *and* VIOLET*)* And I don't even like you people all that much. *(Pause. Silence. He lets that sink in. Then:)* Francis—gently, but firmly, restrain Miss Rose.

*(*FRANCIS *does so.)*

BILLY: Hey!

ROSE: Get your big fat hands off of me!

RAY: Boss, please, I mean my sister…

(BILLY *lunges at* FRANCIS, *but* BIG BOSSMAN *hits him across the head with his walking stick.* BILLY *falls to the floor.* RAY *freezes.* BILLY *is holding his head, stunned.* BIG BOSSMAN *stands over him, with his cane raised.*)

FRANCIS: Francis has hands that are strong. Not fat.

BIG BOSSMAN: Ray?

RAY: Yes?

BIG BOSSMAN: Ray, what is the capital of Venezuela?

RAY: What?

BIG BOSSMAN: The capital of Venezuela?

RAY: Uh…I…

BIG BOSSMAN: I'm asking you a question, Ray.

RAY: Uh, yes sir…

BIG BOSSMAN: Well?

RAY: I don't know the answer to that, sir.

BIG BOSSMAN: You don't?

RAY: No.

BIG BOSSMAN: Pity.

(BIG BOSSMAN *whacks* BILLY *with his cane.* BILLY *yells in pain, rolls around a little, too stunned to do anything.*)

ROSE: Don't you touch him! You fuck! You stupid intruding interloping jack-rabbit fuck!

BIG BOSSMAN: Language!

RAY: Boss, sir, please…!

BIG BOSSMAN: The answer is Caracas. Here's an easy one. Capital of Brazil.

RAY: Uh…uh…

BIG BOSSMAN: Yes?

RAY: Rio!

BIG BOSSMAN: Rio what? Rio Grande?

RAY: Rio de Janeiro!

BIG BOSSMAN: *(Smiles slowly:)* Wrong. *(He whacks* BILLY *again.)*

ROSE: Goddamnit! You scumbag! You fat-headed "I'm such a gentleman look at me I'm a yuppie Sidney Greenstreet ain't I slick like Kaiser Soze, but I'm really just a scuzzy violent punk who got fucked in the ass by a two-hundred-fifty pound white supremacist the last time I did a five-year stretch up-state!"

BIG BOSSMAN: The answer is Brasilia. Next question: Who was the twenty-first president of the United States?

RAY: Ahhh…

BIG BOSSMAN: We haven't got all day.

RAY: Wait, I…I'm counting…

BIG BOSSMAN: Your time is running out, Ray.

ROSE: It's…

RAY: William McKinley!

ROSE: Oh, Ray…

BIG BOSSMAN: Wrong. *(He whacks* BILLY *again.)* The answer is, Chester A Arthur. Next question. This one's easy. The thirtieth president of the United States.

ROSE: Calvin Coolidge!

BIG BOSSMAN: Calvin Coolidge is correct, but your answer is disqualified, Miss Rose. You are not a contestant, and Ray did not ask for a lifeline.

FRANCIS: The Bossman contends that your state of contestitude is highly spurious and furthermore utterly misbegotten.

RAY: Can I ask for a lifeline?

BIG BOSSMAN: In point of fact, you cannot. *(He whacks Billy again.)*

RAY: Boss, please!

ROSE: What the fuck was that for?

BIG BOSSMAN: A penalty for interference, Ma'am. I recommend that you do not answer for Ray again.

FRANCIS: The Bossman respectfully requisitions that you refrain from imposing rejoinders to inquisitions not directed at you directly.

BIG BOSSMAN: Next question: The ninth president of the United States.

(Long pause. RAY stands with his eyes shut tight, concentrating. Finally:)

RAY: William Harrison!!!

(Beat. BIG BOSSMAN smiles at RAY.)

BIG BOSSMAN: Correct.

RAY: I knew that 'cause I remembered that he didn't live too long.

BIG BOSSMAN: Neither will your brother, Ray.

(Suddenly, BILLY smacks BIG BOSSMAN a good one in the crotch. BIG BOSSMAN falls back and drops his cane. He supports himself from falling with the table, gasping for breathe. FRANCIS throws ROSE to the floor, and pulls out a pistol. BILLY crawls away, still too stunned to stand up. RAY pulls at his own hair. FRANCIS keeps everyone covered.)

ROSE: You walk in here all natty and pretentious, like you're some kind of Donald Trump, but you're nothing more than a polished-up street-hustler and a bargain-basement discount pimp!

RAY: Rose, please let me handle this…

ROSE: Let you handle this! You don't even know who Calvin Coolidge was, you idiot!

RAY: I knew who he was! I just didn't know his number!

ROSE: *(To* BIG BOSSMAN*)* You call yourself an entrepreneur? You have the temerity to call yourself the Boss? You have the gall to call yourself a leader? A leader among men? You're a coward and a bully, Mister!

BIG BOSSMAN: Francis! Please hand me that gun.

*(*FRANCIS *does so.)*

VIOLET: You are a brute, Boss. And I never liked you.

BIG BOSSMAN: Violet, I did not purchase you to like me.

VIOLET: You don't know the first thing about me, Boss.

BIG BOSSMAN: That, likewise, has nothing to do with our business together, Violet.

VIOLET: *(To the others in the room:)* He's such a smooth operator.

BILLY: *(Hurt and crumpled on the floor:)* I know all the Presidents, Boss. In chronological order. All forty-something of them.

BIG BOSSMAN: *(Sits on the edge of the table, wipes his forehead with a handkerchief, the gun in his other hand.)* Not for much longer, Billy, not for much longer.

RAY: Ummm…can't we work this out, sir?

BIG BOSSMAN: Who do you work for, Ray?

RAY: I work for you, sir.

BIG BOSSMAN: What does that mean, Ray?

RAY: That means that you're my boss, sir.

BIG BOSSMAN: But, do you know what that means?

RAY: What it means that you're my boss?

BIG BOSSMAN: Yes.

RAY: That I…do what you say, sir.

BIG BOSSMAN: Exactly so, Ray. Exactly so. *(Beat)* Get undressed.

RAY: What?

BIG BOSSMAN: Get undressed. Like Violet was earlier this evening.

(Pause. RAY *starts to get undressed.)*

BILLY: George Washington, John Adams, Thomas Jefferson, James Madison, James Monroe, John Quincy Adams…

RAY: What do you want me to do, sir?

BILLY: Andrew Jackson, Martin Van Buren, William Henry Harrison, John Tyler, James K Polk, Zachary Taylor…

RAY: What is it that you want me to do, sir?

BILLY: Milard Filmore, Franklin Pierce, James Buchanan, "Honest" Abraham Lincoln, Andrew Johnson, Ulysses S Grant…

RAY: What is it that you would have me do, Boss?

BILLY: Rutherford B Hayes, James A Garfield, Chester A Arthur, Grover Cleveland, Benjamin Harrison, Grover Cleveland, William Mckinley…

BIG BOSSMAN: What did Billy do to your Boss, just now?

BILLY: Theodore Roosevelt, William H Taft, Woodrow Wilson, Warren G Harding, Calvin Coolidge, Herbert Hoover…

RAY: He hit you in the nuts, sir.

BILLY: Franklin D Roosevelt, "Give 'em Hell" Harry S Truman, Dwight D "Ike" Eisenhower, John Fitzgerald Kennedy…

BIG BOSSMAN: Is that acceptable, Ray?

BILLY: Lyndon Banes Johnson, Richard Milhous Nixon…

RAY: Uhhh… No?

BILLY: Gerald R Ford, James E Carter Jr, Ronald Wilson Reagan, George Herbert Walker Bush, William Jefferson Clinton, George W Bush, Barack Hussein Obama!

BIG BOSSMAN: No. It isn't. Certainly not.

(By this time, RAY *is in his underwear.)*

BIG BOSSMAN: The rest, please.

RAY: Boss…my *sister*.

BIG BOSSMAN: The rest.

(Beat. RAY *drops his shorts, and stands there, naked.)*

BIG BOSSMAN: How do you feel, Ray?

(Beat)

RAY: Cold?

(Beat)

BIG BOSSMAN: People—people like you, Ray—they think, I will do a job and contract my labor and be paid an agreed upon amount in return. But this thinking is shit, Ray. This is a fantasy. You do not own your labor. I own your labor. And I own the wealth your labor produces. I own it because that is the way of the world. Great men own the fruits of the labors of lesser men. You have no rights to your labor, you have no rights to anything. I pay you what I feel like paying you. This is why, Ray, when men like me stuffed the American economy into the toilet, took a shit on it, and flushed it down the pipe, the Government ran in to bail us out, make us whole, and provide us with hand-jobs for good measure. The economy is hemorrhaging three quarters of a million jobs a month, but men like me are raking it in hand over fist while men like you cannot put together enough to pay the rent. You are my bitch, Ray. Every bit as much as Violet is. Every bit as much as Miranda was. I could make you dance a jig if I wanted to. I could fuck you in front of your entire family, were I so inclined. I could tatoo my brand on your ass, if I so choose. I could suck out your eyeballs and skull fuck your brains, Ray. Everyone in this room is my bitch. Even your sister, Rose. I could strip her naked, too, just like you. I could carve my initials on her tits. I could fuck her right in front of you. I could make you fuck her in right in front of me and your entire family. Right now. I think I will.

(Beat)

RAY: Please don't.

BIG BOSSMAN: I think I will. Fuck your sister, Ray.

RAY: Please.

BIG BOSSMAN: Then fuck your brother. Fuck them both. *(He offers* RAY *his walking stick.)* With this.

RAY: Boss.

BIG BOSSMAN: Now.

(Beat)

*(*RAY *moves towards* BIG BOSSMAN *to take the walking stick.)*

BIG BOSSMAN: What the fuck are you doing, you degenerate, what's wrong with you?

RAY: But—

BIG BOSSMAN: I've changed my mind. Because I can do that. I can do whatever I want to, Ray. Because everyone is my bitch. Do you understand that? Do you, Ray?

(Beat)

RAY: Yes.

(Beat)

BIG BOSSMAN: Good.

(BIG BOSSMAN *hands* RAY *his pistol.*)

(Beat)

BILLY: I can also name each and every one of the Vice-Presidents, also in chronological order.

RAY: What do you want me to do, sir?

ROSE: I thought you said every family could ride above it's station.

BIG BOSSMAN: I lied.

BILLY: John Adams, Thomas Jefferson, Aaron Burr, George Clinton, George Clinton, Elbridge Gerry…

RAY: What do you want me to do?

BIG BOSSMAN: I think that you already know.

BILLY: Daniel D Tompkins, John C Calhoun, John C Calhoun, Martin Van Buren, Richard M. Johnson…

RAY: Tell me.

BILLY: John Tyler, George M Dallas, Millard Fillmore, William R King, John C Breckinridge, Hannibal Hamlin, Andrew Johnson.

BIG BOSSMAN: Go to your brother.

(RAY *does so.*)

BILLY: Schuyler Colfax, Henry Wilson, William A Wheeler, Chester A Arthur, Thomas A Hendricks…

BIG BOSSMAN: Put the gun to your brother's head.

(RAY *does so.*)

ROSE: Ray…

BILLY: *(Faster:)* Levi P Morton, Adlai E Stevenson, Garret A Hobart, Theodore Roosevelt, Charles W Fairbanks...

BIG BOSSMAN: Right at the nape of his neck.

(RAY does so.)

BILLY: *(Faster:)* James S Sherman, Thomas R Marshall, Calvin Coolidge, Charles G Dawes, Charles Curtis...

BIG BOSSMAN: Pull the trigger.

ROSE: No, please—

BILLY: *(Faster:)* John N Garner, Henry A Wallace, Harry S Truman, Alben W Barkley, Richard M Nixon...

RAY: Please don't make me do this, sir.

BILLY: *(Faster:)* Lyndon B Johnson, Hubert H Humphrey, Spiro T Agnew, Gerald R Ford, Nelson A Rockefeller, Walter F Mondale, George H W Bush, James Danforth Quayle, Albert Arnold Gore, Richard Bruce Cheney, Joseph Robinette Biden, Jr!

ROSE: Boss. Please.

(Beat)

BIG BOSSMAN: Do it.

(Beat)

BILLY: I can also name, in chronological order, the runners-up in each presidential election.

BIG BOSSMAN: Pull the trigger.

BILLY: John Adams, John Adams, Thomas Jefferson, Aaron Burr, Charles C Pinkney, Charles C Pinkney, De Witt Clinton...

BIG BOSSMAN: Do as I say.

BILLY: Rufus King, no opposition, Andrew Jackson, John Quincy Adams, Henry Clay, William Henry Harrison, Martin Van Buren...

BIG BOSSMAN: Pull the trigger.

BILLY: Henry Clay, Lewis Cass, Winfield Scott, John C Fremont, Stephen A Douglas, George B McClellan…

BIG BOSSMAN: I AM YOUR BOSS.

BILLY: Horatio Seymour, Horace Greeley, Samuel J Tilden, Winfield S Hancock, James G Blaine…

BIG BOSSMAN: YOU WILL DO AS I SAY.

BILLY: Grover Cleveland, Benjamin Harrison, William Jennings Bryan, William Jennings Bryan…

BIG BOSSMAN: I PAY YOUR WAGES.

BILLY: Alton B Parker, William Jennings Bryan, Theodore Roosevelt—

BIG BOSSMAN: I KEEP YOU ANIMATE.

BILLY: Charles E Hughes, James M Cox…

BIG BOSSMAN: YOU OWE ME ALLEGIANCE.

BILLY: John W Davis…

BIG BOSSMAN: SHOOT HIM NOW.

BILLY: Alfred E Smith!

BIG BOSSMAN: PULL THE TRIGGER.

BILLY: Herbert Hoover!

BIG BOSSMAN: SPLATTER HIS BRAINS ACROSS THE FLOOR.

BILLY: Alfred M Landon!

BIG BOSSMAN: SHOOT HIM.

BILLY: WENDELL L WILKIE!

BIG BOSSMAN: KILL HIM CLEVER, KILL HIM QUICK.

BILLY: THOMAS E DEWEY!

BIG BOSSMAN: KILL HIM FOR ME, RAY.

BILLY: THOMAS E DEWEY!

BIG BOSSMAN: FOR YOUR BOSS, RAY.

BILLY: ADLAI E STEVENSON!

BIG BOSSMAN: FOR THE BIG GUY, RAY.

BILLY: ADLAI E STEVENSON!

BIG BOSSMAN: DO ME THAT COURTESY, RAY.

BILLY: RICHARD M NIXON!

BIG BOSSMAN: IT'S THE LEAST THAT YOU CAN DO!

BILLY: BARRY M GOLDWATER!

BIG BOSSMAN: IT'S THE LEAST THAT I DESERVE!

BILLY: HUBERT H HUMPHREY!

BIG BOSSMAN: AFTER ALL I'VE DONE FOR YOU!

BILLY: GEORGE S McGOVERN!

BIG BOSSMAN: DO IT, RAY!

BILLY: GERALD R FORD!

BIG BOSSMAN: PULL THE TRIGGER!

BILLY: JAMES E CARTER JR!

ROSE: No, God, no, please, whatever you want, please, just don't hurt him, please!

BIG BOSSMAN: KILL YOUR BROTHER FOR ME, RAY!

BILLY: WALTER F MONDALE! MICHAEL STANLEY DUKAKIS! GEORGE H W BUSH! ROBERT JOSEPH DOLE! ALBERT ARNOLD GORE! JOHN FORBES KERRY! JOHN SIDNEY MCCAIN III!

(Beat)

BIG BOSSMAN: NOW.

(Beat)

(Enter CURTIS, *in bathrobe and pajamas. He carries a bottle of whiskey. He looks around.)*

CURTIS: Did I hear someone mention Wendell Wilkie?

(Everyone turns to look at him.)

(Long pause. BIG BOSSMAN *stares hard at* CURTIS. *There is a scary moment before we know what* BIG BOSSMAN *is going to do. Then, he responds, as if everything were normal.)*

BIG BOSSMAN: I think Billy did indeed mention Wendell Wilkie, sir.

CURTIS: *(Looks over at* BILLY *and* RAY:*)* Billy, get up off the floor!

*(*RAY *takes the gun away from* BILLY's *neck and helps him up, then takes* BILLY *to a chair, away from the table and* BIG BOSSMAN.*)*

CURTIS: And Ray, put away that gun before you hurt yourself!

*(*RAY *looks around trying to figure out what to do with the gun.* FRANCIS *extends his hand.* RAY *gives it to him.)*

CURTIS: And for heaven's sake, what are you doing gallivanting around in front of company completely bare-assed? Put something on!

*(*RAY *looks at the* BIG BOSSMAN *for permission. The* BIG BOSSMAN *stares back without commitment, but then finally nods his acquiescence.* RAY *starts to get dressed.)*

CURTIS: And Rose, will you leave that young man alone?

(Beat. FRANCIS *looks at* BIG BOSSMAN. BIG BOSSMAN *nods.* FRANCIS *releases* ROSE.*)*

ROSE: *(To* BIG BOSSMAN:*)* BITE ME!

CURTIS: Rose, that's no way to speak to a guest.

ROSE: He's not a guest!

*(*ROSE *goes to* BILLY *to attend to his injuries.)*

CURTIS: He is in my house and that makes him a guest!

ROSE: *(To* RAY:*)* And you! What were you going to do if he'd insisted you go through with it?

RAY: Which part? The part with Billy or the part with… the cane?

ROSE: Either! Both!

RAY: I wouldn't have done it. Either one. No way.

BIG BOSSMAN: Liar.

ROSE: *(To* BIG BOSSMAN*)* I wasn't talking to you! Fuck off!

CURTIS: Rose! That will be quite enough of that! *(To* BIG BOSSMAN:*)* My name is Curtis, sir.

BIG BOSSMAN: Pleased to meet you, Mister Curtis.

CURTIS: Just Curtis.

BIG BOSSMAN: Pleased to meet you, Curtis.

CURTIS: The pleasure is mine. *(To* VIOLET:*)* And who may you be, young lady?

VIOLET: I may be Violet, sir.

CURTIS: You may indeed. Pleased to have made your acquaintance, Miss Violet.

VIOLET: And pleased to have made yours, sir.

CURTIS: *(To* BIG BOSSMAN:*)* I remember Wendell Wilkie, Mister.

BIG BOSSMAN: You do?

CURTIS: Yes, indeed I do. 1940 Republican Presidential candidate.

RAY: Dad?

CURTIS: Yes, son?

RAY: What are you doing out of bed?

CURTIS: I am speaking to our guest.

RAY: You haven't been out of bed in, like, years.

CURTIS: Oh, that. I fell asleep watching a gameshow—
Surviving Chains of Love and Death, I think it was called.
It involved a series of couples, men and women. Each
couple was stripped naked, chained at the ankles,
and sent off to fend for themselves on a hostile, jungle
island. They were also chased by professional hunters,
with high powered rifles. If a hunter caught a couple,
they shot the male, and had his head mounted in the
hunter's lodge. At the end of every week, the females
whose males had been shot were eaten by the other
contestants. Also, when two couples met in the jungle,
the two men fought to the death. The winner claimed
the female. Her chain was attached to his, so then he
had two females chained to his ankles. The idea was,
the man who had the most women chained to him won
the game. But the trick was, the more women a man
had chained to his ankles, the easier target he was for
the hunters with their high-powered rifles. *(Beat)* There
was this one little lady, though. Real spitfire. Her mate
was killed by another man, and then she turned the
tables and killed that man. Killed his mate, too. Bashed
'em both in the head with a rock. Then she chewed off
the arm of her dead mate, and she took to the jungle
by herself, trying to avoid the hunters and the other
couples. Turned out, at the end, she was the only one
left standing. *(Beat)* She didn't win the million bucks,
though. She was disqualified. Didn't play by the rules
of the game. *(Beat)* Then, I fell asleep and I had a little
dream. Stirred me up. *(Beat. To* BIG BOSSMAN*)* Care to
join me for some fortification, Mister?

BIG BOSSMAN: That's very kind of you indeed, Curtis.

CURTIS: ROSE! Get us some glasses!

ROSE: I will do no such thing!

CURTIS: Rose, I would like to have a drink with my new friend here! We need glasses in order to make that happen in a satisfactory and well-mannered fashion.

ROSE: He's a thug and a brute, Dad! I won't have him drinking in our house!

CURTIS: You are just being plain rude!

ROSE: I don't care! I won't have him beneath our roof!

CURTIS: And since when have you been the boss of this household!

ROSE: SINCE YOU DECIDED TO TAKE TO YOUR BED AND SUCK ON A BOTTLE OF ROTGUT LIKE IT WAS YOUR MOTHER'S TIT!

(A very long pause as ROSE *and* CURTIS *stare at one another,* ROSE *with defiance,* CURTIS *with murder in his eyes.)*

VIOLET: *(Finally breaking the tension and bringing two glasses over:)* Here ya' go.

BIG BOSSMAN: Thank you, Violet.

*(*ROSE *and* CURTIS *are still facing one another off. Beat)*

BIG BOSSMAN: How about that drink, Curtis?

*(*CURTIS *and* ROSE *face off a moment longer.)*

CURTIS: *(Finally breaking from* ROSE:*)* Sure thing, Mister.

*(*CURTIS *fills the glasses, hands one to* BIG BOSSMAN, *who takes a seat.* CURTIS *takes a seat by him. Throughout the room, everyone finally takes a somewhat more relaxed posture, keeping distance between themselves and the center table.* ROSE *attends to some of* BILLY's *bruises.* VIOLET *stands aside.)*

BIG BOSSMAN: What is this dream you had, Curtis?

CURTIS: Pardon?

BIG BOSSMAN: The dream that brought you out of bed.

CURTIS: Oh, that. I dreamed I was in a room.

(Beat)

BIG BOSSMAN: Interesting.

CURTIS: With Wendell Wilkie and Franklin Delano Roosevelt.

BIG BOSSMAN: The plot thickens.

CURTIS: They were both lighting cigars and tossing them at one another. Joe Stalin and Winston Churchill were also there, standin' in the corner, spittin' tobacco juice at one another. Roosevelt started zipping around in his wheel-chair, smackin' everybody else in the room with a baseball bat. Stalin took out a pistol and tried to shoot Roosevelt, but he kept missin'. Churchill and Wilkie were drinkin' wine and dancing around, singing Yiddish folk songs. Charles de Gaulle walked in and dropped his pants. Stalin tried to shoot him, too, but he kept missin'. De Gaulle started walkin' around like a chicken and makin' anti-Semitic remarks. Churchill and Wilkie tried to look offended. Roosevelt was takin' his wheelchair up and down the walls by now. Stalin' announced that he was gonna sing the entire Kris Kristofferson songbook. He burst into *Me and Bobbie McGee*, singing in a heavy Russian accent. He followed that up with *Help Me Make it Through the Night*, and everyone joined in. De Gaulle got angry 'cause he didn't know the words, so he launched into the *Marseillaise*. Roosevelt, who by now was zipping back and forth on the ceiling, got angry and started smacking de Gaulle in the head with the baseball bat. Just then, in walks Hitler, and everybody stops what they're doing and walks around trying to ignore him, all holdin' their noses and complaining about a bad smell. Hitler gets angry and pees in the corner, and then proceeds to attempt to sing the entire Cole Porter catalogue. He get's through *You're the Top* alright, but

forgets the words to *Begin the Beguine,* so he gives up
and just sits in his own piss, sulking. Roosevelt starts
pelting him with pistachio nuts from his position on
the ceiling. De Gaulle starts flappin' his arms like he's
tryin' to fly. Alf Landon shows up then and starts
spinning around in a circle. Churchill and Wilkie are
doing Greek dances at this point. Stalin's trying to
blow Alf Landon away with the pistol, but he keeps
missin'. Hitler gets fed up with Roosevelt's barrage of
pistachio nuts, so he stands up and tries to pee on him.
But Hitler can't reach that high up to the ceiling, and
winds up pissing all over Stalin's back. Stalin's furious.
He turns around slowly with his face turning beet red.
Hitler's terrified 'cause Stalin's so much bigger than
him. Stalin takes careful aim and fires all six rounds
at Hitler. They all miss. Stalin blows his top and starts
huckin' furniture at him. Hitler cowers in the corner,
with chairs and tables and desks bouncing off his head.
By now, Alf Landon has joined de Gaulle in flapping
his arms like he's trying to take off. Roosevelt starts
pelting them both with pistachio nuts. Churchill and
Wilkie start to tango, and get in an argument over
who gets to lead. *(Beat)* At that point I left the room.
I walked down the hall. I walked outside. All around
me was rubble and ruin. Ancient stone European
castles reduced to scattered pebbles, next to modern
apartment houses riddled with bullet holes, entire
walls torn out, roofs on the verge of collapse, pipes and
twisted plumbing hanging there, like the intestines of
a disemboweled cow. In the center of all this, a little
girl in a tattered dress was skipping rope. I stood there
and watched her as she sang the entire Stephen Foster
catalogue.

(A beat as everyone looks at CURTIS, *stunned.)*

BIG BOSSMAN: Quite a dream, Curtis.

CURTIS: Was a humdinger, wasn't it, Mister?

(Beat)

VIOLET: I know a Stephen Foster song.

CURTIS: Do you?

VIOLET: Yes.

CURTIS: Will you sing it for us?

VIOLET: Oh, I couldn't.

CURTIS: I'm sure that you could.

VIOLET: I'm not prepared.

CURTIS: Who needs to be prepared to sing? You just open your mouth and unleash your throat.

VIOLET: But I've got no accompaniment.

CURTIS: Who needs it? Pianos are over-rated. The art of song is about the unadorned human voice vibrating the molecules of the air. Sing.

VIOLET: Well…

CURTIS: C'mon…

VIOLET: I don't know…

CURTIS: Please?

(Beat)

VIOLET: Well…okay… *(She takes center-stage and sings Foster's* Hard Times, *beautifully, with feeling:)*
Let us pause in life's pleasures, and count its many
   tears
While we all sup sorrow with the poor.
There's a song that will linger forever in our ears
Oh, hard times, come again no more.

'Tis the song, the sigh of the weary
Hard times, hard times, come again no more
Many days you have lingered around my cabin door
Oh, hard times come again no more.

(Suddenly, FRANCIS, clearly and deeply moved, joins in. He, too, sings beautifully:)

FRANCIS & VIOLET:
'Tis a sigh that is wafted, across the troubled wave
'Tis a wail that is heard upon the shore
'Tis a dirge that is murmured around the lowly grave
Oh, hard times come again no more

'Tis the song, the sigh of the weary
Hard times, hard times come again no more
Many days you have lingered around my cabin door
Oh, hard times, come again no more.

(FRANCIS takes the next part alone, as VIOLET hums accompaniment:)

FRANCIS: While we seek mirth and beauty, and music
    light and gay
There are frail forms fainting at the door
Tho' their voices are silent, their pleading looks will
    say
Oh, hard times come again no more

'Tis the song, the sigh of the weary
Hard times, hard times come again no more
Many days you have lingered around my cabin door
Oh, hard times, come again no more.

FRANCIS & VIOLET: There's a pale drooping maiden
    who toils her life away,
With a worn heart whose better days are o'er:
Though her voice would be merry, 'tis sighing all the
    day,
Oh hard times come again no more.

'Tis the song, the sigh of the weary
Hard times, hard times come again no more
Many days you have lingered around my cabin door
Oh, hard times, come again no more.

(Great applause all around. FRANCIS *and* VIOLET *smile and bow to the people in the room one at a time. They make a big show of it, holding hands and taking turns like opera singers.)*

(Then VIOLET *reaches into* FRANCIS's *coat, pulls out the gun he had taken from* RAY, *and shoots* FRANCIS *dead.)*

CURTIS: Violet! That was a horribly, terribly, grotesquely unneighborly thing to do!

*(*VIOLET *shoots* BIG BOSSMAN *in the gut. He falls on the floor, gasping for air.)*

CURTIS: VIOLET! THIS WHOLE THING IS GETTING TOTALLY OUT OF HAND!

VIOLET: Who is the bitch now, Bossman?

BIG BOSSMAN: CUNT! GODDAMN UNGRATEFUL CUNT!

VIOLET: You're the only cunt in the room I can see!

CURTIS: Language!

BIG BOSSMAN: BITCH!

CURTIS: Quiet, Mister, I'm trying to teach this lady some manners!

ROSE: Oh my God!

BIG BOSSMAN: FRANCIS!

RAY: *(To* BILLY:*)* See what you've done!

BILLY: Sorry.

BIG BOSSMAN: FRANCIS, GET ME OUT OF HERE!

CURTIS: Quiet, Mister! Francis can't help you!

BIG BOSSMAN: FRANCIS!!!!!!

CURTIS: Mister! Have some respect for the dead!

BIG BOSSMAN: Do you know what you have done? I mean, don't you know who I am? Don't you realize the consequences? I can walk barefoot over broken glass and people will jump in my path so I can walk upon their backs, because they are so afraid of the consequences of my unhappiness! This kind of thing does not happen to a man like me! It just doesn't happen! This isn't right! It isn't right!

(Beat)

VIOLET: *(To the family:)* Look, I'm really sorry about this and everything.

CURTIS: Well, I should hope that you are!

VIOLET: I am. I'm really sorry for any inconvenience or mental stress I might have caused you. But it really seemed like it was the only thing to do.

CURTIS: It was a little bit extravagant, if you ask me!

(As she speaks, VIOLET starts to rummage in FRANCIS's pockets until she finds what she is looking for—the grotesquely fat money clip he carries for BIG BOSSMAN.)

VIOLET: No, really. I don't think that there was any other way out. I don't think there's any way to hide from a problem. I think you've got to face it head-on.

CURTIS: What is this, self-help philosophy? Pretty lame, if you ask me!

VIOLET: No. It's not self-help. Well, maybe it is. I needed help. I helped myself. Simple as that.

CURTIS: SURE IT'S SIMPLE! THAT STILL DOESN'T MAKE IT NICE!

VIOLET: I never said it was nice.

CURTIS: WELL, DON'T KID YOURSELF, MISSY, 'CAUSE IT AIN'T!

VIOLET: I just said that it was necessary.

CURTIS: A PRETTY POOR EXCUSE FOR THIS KIND OF BEHAVIOR, IF YOU ASK ME!

VIOLET: Look, I'm really sorry. Really, I am. I don't
do this kind of thing often, y'know. I feel really bad
comin' in here and disrupting everything, and getting
Billy all beat up like that, and then shooting these two
to boot. I know it makes things awkward for you.
Believe me, if there'd been any other way, I wouldn't
have done it. *(Beat)* Look, if you want me to stick
around clean up the mess, I'll do it. A little ammonia
and Lysol should do the trick. *(Beat)* Well, I'd better be
going. Thanks for your help, Billy.

(Beat)

BILLY: Anytime.

VIOLET: Thanks for the tea, Rose.

ROSE: No problem, Violet.

VIOLET: Sorry it had to turn out his way. Best of luck
to all of you. I mean that. I really do. *(Beat)* Oh, by
the way, it was *The Green Berets*. The other film John
Wayne directed. 1968-ish. Vietnam film. *The Alamo*
wasn't the only one. Wayne directed *The Green Berets*,
too.

BILLY: David Jansen was in that one.

VIOLET: That's right. *The Green Berets*. Well. *(She puts
some money on the table.)* For your troubles. *(Beat)* 'Bye.

(VIOLET exits. Beat)

RAY: Well, now we're out of a job, that's for sure.

BIG BOSSMAN: Not…necessarily…

RAY: *(To BILLY:)* You see where being helpful to whores
gets you, Billy? All that fuss, all that sturm and all
that drang and look what happens! You call this some
kind of, what, an achievement? This is no kind of an
achievement! This is just plain messy! What're we
gonna do now? Bodies all over the place!

ROSE: Quiet! Let me think!

CURTIS: Well, this is really a fine way to run a household, I can tell you that!

ROSE: Everything was fine until you had to bring up Stephen Foster!

CURTIS: Stephen Foster has never driven anyone to commit an act of violence! If it hadn't been Stephen Foster it would've been George Gershwin! When you let riff-raff like that into your house, you never know what will happen!

ROSE: Oh, sure, now she's riff-raff, but when you first saw her it was all you could do to keep from drooling!

CURTIS: Don't you talk to your father that way! I say she's riff-raff!

BILLY: Oh, what d'you care anyway?

CURTIS: Not a lick, son, not a rat's ass! WHERE'S MY FORTIFICATION?

ROSE: FIND IT YOURSELF!

(Beat)

CURTIS: Has this household gone completely out of bounds? Have we finally gone off the deep end? Entered another dimension? Hit the last stage of familial de-evolution? Is that what we have done? Because if it is, then I'd sure as Hell like to know about it! I MEAN, COULD SOMEONE INFORM ME, JUST SO I CAN PROCEED ACCORDINGLY?

ROSE: Oh, shut up.

CURTIS: THIS PLACE HAS NOTHING TO DO WITH A HOUSE AT ALL! THIS PLACE IS NOT A HOME! WE ARE NOT A FAMILY! WE ARE A BUNCH OF PEOPLE IN THE SAME ROOM WHO DON'T LIKE EACH OTHER VERY MUCH!

ROSE: WELL! YOU FINALLY NOTICED!

BIG BOSSMAN: I like…you…all…really…

ROSE: QUIET! THERE'S BLOOD IN THIS HOUSE!
THERE'S DEATH IN THIS HOUSE! THERE HAS
NEVER BEEN DEATH IN THIS HOUSE BEFORE!

CURTIS: THE DEATH OF THIS FAMILY! THERE'S
BEEN THAT!

ROSE: DON'T BE MELODRAMATIC!

BILLY: Mother died.

ROSE: What?

BILLY: Mother died in this house.

ROSE: SHE DIED IN THE HOSPITAL! SHE DID NOT
DIE UNDER THIS ROOF!

BILLY: She did. She died in her bed.

CURTIS: YOU LEAVE YOUR MOTHER OUT OF THIS,
GOD REST HER SOUL!

BIG BOSSMAN: WILL SOMEBODY PLEASE HELP
ME?!?

ROSE: BE QUIET! YOU'RE BETTER OFF THAN
FRANCIS, THAT'S FOR SURE!

BIG BOSSMAN: That's not very comforting…

BILLY: Maybe we should do something…

RAY: LIKE WHAT FOR INSTANCE? SECURE
ALTERNATE EMPLOYMENT? JOBS ARE NOT THAT
EASY TO COME BY, Y'KNOW! JOBS ARE NOT A
DIME A DOZEN! JOBS ARE PRETTY DAMN SCARCE
THESE DAYS, AS A MATTER OF FACT!

BILLY: I wasn't talking about a job…

RAY: WE'RE LIVING IN A SERVICE ECONOMY
NOW, Y'KNOW THAT? Y'KNOW WHAT "SERVICE
ECONOMY" MEANS? IT MEANS GET A JOB AT
MCDONALD'S AND SHUT YOUR FACE! THAT'S

WHAT IT MEANS! THAT'S WHAT OUR OPTIONS ARE NOW, BILLY!

ROSE: We're not living in a service economy! We're living in the information age!

RAY: OH! WELL! NOW, I FEEL COMFORTED! I MEAN, I'LL JUST PUT MY SOFTWARE DESIGNING SKILLS TO USE, OR MAYBE BILLY CAN START WRITING SOME BINARY CODE! HOW ABOUT IT, BILLY? THINK YOU CAN USE THOSE COMPUTERS AT THE LIBRARY FOR SOMETHING OTHER THAN DOWNLOADING PORN? YOU REALLY DON'T KNOW WHEN YOU'VE GOT A GOOD THING GOING, DO YOU?

BILLY: You can't download porn at the library. They got one of them v-chip blocker programs going.

ROSE: Where'd you learn that, "service economy"? "Binary Code"?

RAY: I heard it on National Public Radio!

CURTIS: Oh, my! Well, aren't we just so hoity AND toity! National Public Radio! *All Things Considered*, I bet!

RAY: What if it was?

CURTIS: That's a Communist program, and I won't have you listening to that propaganda!

ROSE: It's not a Communist program, Dad. There are no Communists anymore, don't you know that?

RAY: He would if he listened to National Public Radio!

CURTIS: I haven't watched the news or read a paper since Nixon resigned! And I don't intend to! Not until they impeach Earl Warren!

RAY: *(To BILLY:)* WELL, NOW YOU'LL SEE, BILLY. YOU'LL SEE HOW YOU LIKE IT WORKING AT MCDONALD'S FOR THE REST OF YOUR LIFE!

THAT'S NOT A JOB WORTHY OF A FAMILY LIKE
US! WE ARE DESCENDED FROM KINGS!

BILLY: I didn't know we were descended from kings...

ROSE: We are not descended from kings. We're
descended from fucking garlic eaters and potato
farmers and ditch diggers and brick layers and bar
tenders and longshoremen and stevedores and cotton
pickers...

RAY: WE ARE DESCENDED FROM KINGS! IF YOU
TRACE IT BACK FAR ENOUGH, ALL YOU GET ARE
KINGS! TONS AND TONS OF KINGS! ENOUGH
KINGS TO FILL A FUCKING STADIUM!

BILLY: I didn't know that.

ROSE: It's not true. He's making it up.

RAY: IRISH KINGS! PERSIAN KINGS! GERMAN
KINGS! RUSSIAN KINGS! ISRAELI KINGS!
ARABIAN KINGS! AFRICAN KINGS! SAMOAN
KINGS! CHINESE KINGS! ICELANDIC KINGS!
AZTEC KINGS! YOU NAME IT!

BIG BOSSMAN: I DON'T CARE WHO YOU ARE
DESCENDED FROM! I AM A KING! A LIVING KING!

CURTIS: Not for much longer.

BIG BOSSMAN: I'M STILL THE BIG BOSSMAN,
GODDAMNIT! I'M STILL IN CHARGE HERE! I'VE
GOT A FUCKING EMPIRE TO BACK ME UP!

CURTIS: With all due respect, Mister, you ain't got
nothin' to back you up now.

BIG BOSSMAN: THE KING IS DEAD! LONG LIVE THE
KING!

CURTIS: That's the spirit.

BILLY: Umm...maybe we should do something?

CURTIS: WE SHOULD GET ME MY FORTIFICATION, THAT'S WHAT WE SHOULD DO!

BIG BOSSMAN: OH MY GOD!

ROSE: FUCK YOU AND YOUR WHISKEY!

CURTIS: THAT DOES IT! I DON'T NEED THIS KIND OF ABUSE! I DON'T HAVE TO PUT UP WITH IT! I USED TO BE SOMETHING, YOU KNOW! I USED TO BE A MAN WHO COMMANDED RESPECT! LIKE THAT MAN LYING ON THE FLOOR THERE USED TO COMMAND RESPECT BEFORE HE GOT GUT-SHOT! YOU THINK I CAN'T BE THAT KIND OF MAN AGAIN? I'LL SHOW YOU! I'LL SHOW YOU ALL! I'M LEAVING!

(CURTIS *exits to his room.*)

BIG BOSSMAN: Ray…Ray…

RAY: WHAT?

BIG BOSSMAN: I can make you an important man, Ray. I can make your family a family of kings again. I can make you a Boss.

RAY: I DON'T WANT TO BE A BOSS! I DON'T CARE ABOUT THAT! I DON'T WANT TO BE A KING! I DON'T WANT TO BE PRESIDENT! IT'S A SUCKY JOB! YOU WIND UP GETTING WASTED BY RENEGADE PROSTITUTES AND MANIAC ANARCHISTS! DO YOU THINK I'VE WORKED THIS HARD TO WIND UP LIKE THAT? I DON'T WANT THAT!

BIG BOSSMAN: Well, what do you want then?

(*Beat*)

RAY: Well… What I want is a house in the suburbs and a handful of kids and a little doggie who shits in the kitchen. I want a Lexus. And a Nexus. And a Nasdaq, and a Dow Jones Average. I want a nice stereo and a pool! I want Blu-ray machine and highspeed internet access.

BILLY: With no V-chip blocking software.

RAY: I want a front lawn with green grass, a white picket fence, and a mailbox with my last name on it. I want to send my kids to college and watch them become doctors and lawyers and bankers and ad executives and Washington lobbyists and Software Tycoons and business entrepreneurs. And when it's all over I want to retire to Florida and when I die I want my ashes fed to the minnows. That's what I want.

BIG BOSSMAN: I...can...get you that...too...

RAY: YOU CAN'T GET ME ANYTHING! YOU DON'T EXIST! YOU ARE VAPOR, BUDDY! YOU HAVEN'T GOT A THING TO OFFER ME!

BIG BOSSMAN: I CAN GIVE YOU ANYTHING YOU WANT!

RAY: LIAR! YOU FUCKING LIAR! THERE WAS A TIME, MAYBE, ONCE UPON A TIME BACK IN THE DAY WHEN A GUY LIKE YOU WOULD GIVE THAT KIND OF STUFF TO A GUY LIKE ME BECAUSE A GUY LIKE ME DID THE STUFF A GUY LIKE YOU NEEDED TO GET DONE! BUT THOSE DAYS ARE OVER. NOW, A GUY LIKE ME JUST GETS CONTINUOUSLY FUCKED IN THE ASS OVER AND OVER AND IS EXPECTED TO SAY THANK YOU FOR THE TABLE SCRAPS A GUY LIKE YOU THROWS MY WAY! WELL FUCK YOU! FUCK YOU AND YOUR FUCKING TABLE SCRAPS! THE ONLY WAY A GUY LIKE ME IS GONNA GET THE THINGS HE DESERVES IS IF HE STOPS BEING A GUY LIKE ME AND STARTS BEING A GUY LIKE YOU BEFORE YOU GOT GUT-SHOT! *(He storms out.)*

(Beat)

BIG BOSSMAN: Rose…?

ROSE: What is it?

BIG BOSSMAN: What is it that you want…?

ROSE: I don't want anything.

BIG BOSSMAN: You must want something!

ROSE: No, really. Nothing.

BIG BOSSMAN: For God's sake, there must be something I can get you!

ROSE: Nope. Thanks anyway.

BIG BOSSMAN: EVERYBODY WANTS SOMETHING! THAT'S THE WHOLE FOUNDATION OF MY SUCCESS! THERE'S NOT A PERSON IN THE WORLD WHO WANTS NOTHING! EVERYBODY WANTS SOMETHING!

ROSE: Not everybody.

BIG BOSSMAN: PLEASE!!!!

ROSE: Look, sir, if there was anything I really wanted, I'd tell you!

BIG BOSSMAN: PLEASE!!!!!

ROSE: You ever been to the Tropics?

BIG BOSSMAN: Of course…

ROSE: What's it like?

BIG BOSSMAN: It's…very nice…

ROSE: *(Wistful:)* Yeah. That's sorta what I figured.

(Beat)

BIG BOSSMAN: BILLY!

BILLY: Yes?

BIG BOSSMAN: WHY, BILLY, WHY?

BILLY: Why what, Boss?

BIG BOSSMAN: WHY DID YOU DO THIS TO ME?

BILLY: I didn't do anything to you, Mister Boss.

BIG BOSSMAN: YOU FUCKED ME UP, BILLY!

BILLY: No. Really. I didn't. I had nothing to do with it. You did it all by yourself.

BIG BOSSMAN: YOU FUCKED ME UP!

BILLY: Well, I didn't exactly pull the trigger or anything.

BIG BOSSMAN: YOU FUCKED ME UP!

BILLY: I didn't smack you with a cane for not knowing the capitals of South American countries or anything...

BIG BOSSMAN: NOBODY FUCKS ME UP, BILLY!

(Beat)

BILLY: Well, somebody did.

(Beat)

BIG BOSSMAN: Billy?

BILLY: Yeah?

BIG BOSSMAN: I miss her.

BILLY: Miranda?

BIG BOSSMAN: I miss her.

BILLY: That story's true?

BIG BOSSMAN: It's true. I miss her. I dream about her.

BILLY: I know where you got the ending, though.

BIG BOSSMAN: What?

BILLY: The ending of your little presentation. "And I don't even like you people that much." It's from *The Long Goodbye*.

BIG BOSSMAN: I don't know what you're talking about.

BILLY: *The Long Goodbye,* 1973, directed by Robert Duvall, written by Leigh Brackett, based on the novel by Raymond Chandler.

BIG BOSSMAN: But my story's true. I didn't get it from a movie. Not even my line at the end. I've never even seen that movie. My story is one hundred percent bona fide. I loved her, Billy. I really, truly did.

BILLY: Yeah, well, if you loved her so much then maybe you shouldn't have cut her face like that, huh?

(Beat)

BIG BOSSMAN: Billy…what can I do, Billy?

BILLY: Do?

BIG BOSSMAN: Can I…make things up to you…?

BILLY: You don't need to make anything up to me.

BIG BOSSMAN: What can I do for your forgiveness, Billy?

BILLY: I've got nothing to forgive you about, Boss.

BIG BOSSMAN: But, I beat you.

BILLY: That doesn't matter.

BIG BOSSMAN: I nearly killed you.

BILLY: That doesn't matter.

BIG BOSSMAN: I would have killed you.

BILLY: It doesn't matter.

BIG BOSSMAN: I would have made Ray kill you.

BILLY: He wouldn't have.

BIG BOSSMAN: Don't be so sure.

BILLY: It doesn't matter.

BIG BOSSMAN: Billy?

BILLY: Yes?

BIG BOSSMAN: What can I do?

(Beat)

BILLY: Nothing.

(Beat)

(CURTIS enters, with suitcase and cane. He is dressed exactly like BIG BOSSMAN.)

CURTIS: I'm leaving.

(Beat. No one replies. CURTIS exits. Beat)

(RAY enters. He also has a suitcase and a cane, and is also dressed exactly like the BIG BOSSMAN.)

RAY: I'm leaving.

(Beat. No one replies. RAY exits. Beat)

ROSE: Billy?

BILLY: Yes?

ROSE: How did you know all those presidents and vice-presidents and runners-up?

BILLY: I had a teacher in Junior High who made me learn them. No one else. Just me. Every time I goofed off in class, he kept me after school and forced me to learn all those names, in chronological order. The whole shebang. Useless stuff. Never liked that teacher. Real creepola. *(Beat)* Turns out it came in kinda handy, though.

(Beat)

(Reprise of the song Big Bossman *is heard, rising in volume as the lights dim.* BILLY *and* ROSE *start to straighten up around the kitchen/living room.* BIG BOSSMAN *lies very still, but still breathing.)*

(The shaft of light from the small, greasy window, begins to shine through.)

(The rest of the lights begin to fade, but that light get brighter and stronger.)

*(*BILLY *and* ROSE *continue to clean up as the lights fade and the shaft of light get brighter.)*

(The song should not be faded out, but allowed to play through to its end, until the stage and house are in total darkness except for the shaft of light from the window.)

(Then, when the song ends, the shaft of light cuts out, abruptly.)

(Curtain)

END OF PLAY